Pray, Hope, & Don't Worry

Women's Prayer Journal For Overcoming Anxiety

A 52-week Guided Devotional
of Prayers & Bible Verses
to Conquer Stress & Fear

Sara A. Smith

Pray, Hope, and Don't Worry
Women's Prayer Journal For Overcoming Anxiety
A 52-week Guided Devotional of Prayers & Bible Verses to Conquer Fear & Stress
Copyright © 2020 Sara A. Smith; Scott L. Smith, editor

ISBN-13: 978-1-950782-15-4
All rights reserved.
Holy Water Books (Publisher)

No part of this book may be reproduced, or stored in a retrieval system, or transmitted in any form or by any means, electronic, mechanical, photocopying, recording, or otherwise, without the express written permission of the author(s) and/or editor(s).

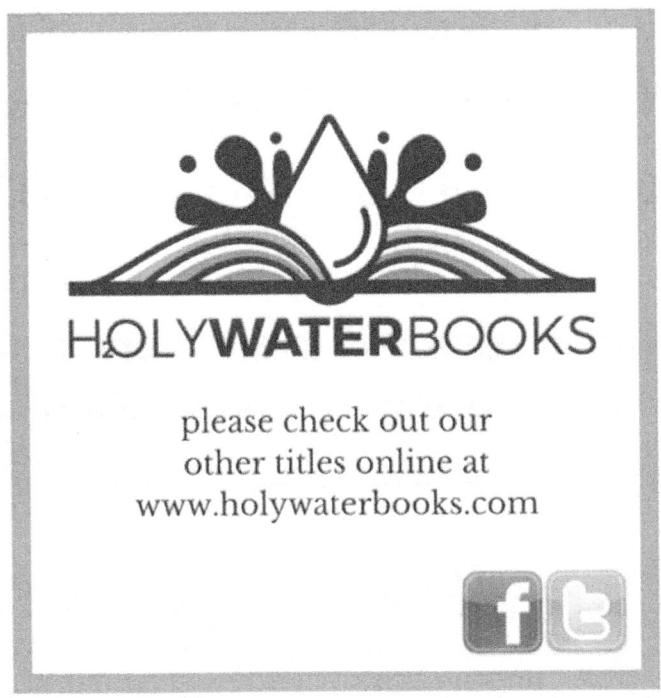

Unless otherwise noted, all quotes from Scripture included in this book are from the Revised Standard Version (RSV).

"Pray, hope, and don't worry.
Worry is useless.
God is merciful and will hear your prayer."

Padre Pio

Table of Contents

Foreward 5

Week One 8

"Take and Receive" Prayer 10

Week Two 12

Act of Hope 14

Week Three 16

Serenity Prayer 18

Week Four 20

Litany of Humility 22

Week Five 24

Prayer for Calm 26

Week Six 28

Litany of Trust, Part One 30

Week Seven 32

Litany of Trust, Part Two 34

Week Eight 36

Prayer for Peace and Calm 38

Week Nine 40

A Prayer for Soothing Panic Attacks 42

Week Ten 44

Your Peace 46

Week Eleven 48

Prayer for Strength 50

Week Twelve 52

Prayer of St. Francis 54

Week Thirteen 56

I Want To Be Available 58
Week Fourteen 60
A Prayer for Calming a Troubled Heart 62
Week Fifteen 64
A Prayer for Christ's Peace 66
Week Sixteen 68
Anima Christi 70
Week Seventeen 72
A Prayer for Hope 74
Week Eighteen 76
A Prayer to Cast Out Fear 78
Week Nineteen 80
A Prayer for the Weary 82
Week Twenty 84
A Prayer for Letting Go of Worries 86
Week Twenty-One 88
Magnificat 90
Week Twenty-Two 92
A Prayer for Unburdening the Mind 94
Week Twenty-Three 96
St. Francis' Canticle of the Sun 98
Week Twenty-Four 100
A Celtic Prayer of Peace 102
Week Twenty-Five 104
Prayer of Saint Richard of Chichester 106
Week Twenty-Six 108
Holy Spirit Prayer of Saint Augustine 110
Week Twenty-Seven 112
"Take and Receive" Prayer 114

Week Twenty-Eight	116
Act of Hope	118
Week Twenty-Nine	120
Serenity Prayer	122
Week Thirty	124
Litany of Humility	126
Week Thirty-One	128
Prayer for Calm	130
Week Thirty-Two	132
Litany of Trust, Part One	134
Week Thirty-Three	136
Litany of Trust, Part Two	138
Week Thirty-Four	140
Prayer for Peace and Calm	142
Week Thirty-Five	144
A Prayer for Soothing Panic Attacks	146
Week Thirty-Six	148
Your Peace	150
Week Thirty-Seven	152
Prayer for Strength	154
Week Thirty-Eight	156
Prayer of St. Francis	158
Week Thirty-Nine	160
I Want To Be Available	162
Week Forty	164
A Prayer for Calming a Troubled Heart	166
Week Forty-One	168
A Prayer for Christ's Peace	170
Week Forty-Two	172

Anima Christi 174

Week Forty-Three 176

A Prayer for Hope 178

Week Forty-Four 180

A Prayer to Cast Out Fear 182

Week Forty-Five 184

A Prayer for the Weary 186

Week Forty-Six 188

A Prayer for 190

Letting Go of Worries 190

Week Forty-Seven 192

Magnificat 194

Week Forty-Eight 196

A Prayer for Unburdening the Mind 198

Week Forty-Nine 200

St. Francis' Canticle of the Sun 202

Week Fifty 204

A Celtic Prayer of Peace 206

Week Fifty-One 208

Prayer of Saint 210

Richard of Chichester 210

Week Fifty-Two 212

Holy Spirit Prayer of 214

Saint Augustine 214

About the Authors 217

Foreword

Welcome to this prayer space!

We hope and pray you will find God here, and He will give you comfort.

There are several **different ways to use this prayer journal**. Though the journal is designed for 52 *weeks* of guided prayer, it could also be used for 52 *days*. Just use each weekly section as a day section, instead. This could also be a resource for Lent if you just use it for 6 weeks or 40 days. We hope this journal will adapt itself to your needs.

Each of the 52 weeks (or days, if you prefer) includes a seven-step prayer sequence. The seven steps are (1) Breathe, (2) Become aware of God's presence, (3) Thanksgiving, (4) Reflect, (5) Examination, (6) Contrition, and (7) Hope. Here is a more in-depth look at the purpose and significance of these steps:

1. The first step, **Breathe**, guides you through a breathing exercise that you can also use whenever you feel stressed, especially when you *first* begin to feel stressed. This breathing exercise can help you ward off a panic attack.
2. Take time to become aware of **God's presence**. Remember that He is closer to you than you are to yourself. He is with you right now, in the *now*. Let your soul come to rest, for as St. Augustine says, "Our hearts were made for You, O Lord, and they are restless until they rest in You."
3. **Thanksgiving:** A key to overcoming anxiety is re-orienting yourself to gratitude. That is, focusing less on your fears and more on God's gifts to you. *Lord, I realize that all, even myself, is a gift from you. Today, for what things am I most grateful?*
4. **Reflect** on the provided verse from Scripture. We chose these verses specifically to help you overcome anxiety. What words stand out to you? What comes into your mind as you reflect on the words? This is the meditative practice of *lectio divina*. Sit with these passages for five minutes or more each day through the week. Plant them in your mind, water them daily with reflection, and let them take root.
5. Ask the Lord to guide you through your day and week. Jesus will take you by the hand to **Examine** the moments and experiences of your life. Wait and see what bubbles up in your memories. What is Jesus trying to reveal to you? Jesus might be saying "I was there in that moment" but you did not see me, feel me, or hear me. Over time, this exercise will help you to know that Jesus never leaves your side and to *sense him* always there.

6. **Contrition**: Big or small, where, when, and how did sin creep into your day? Learning when you are tempted will help you re-route your sin habits toward virtues.
7. Learn to prayerfully anticipate the future in **Hope**. So much of our anxiety comes from unwarranted fear of the future. We dread events that may never come to pass. This exercise will help you shift your focus toward the good that is coming. The ultimate goal is to see God's presence in all things.

A Weekly Prayer is also included. We chose prayers that are focused on overcoming anxiety through gratitude, healing, empowering, and surrendering.

Lastly, each week (or day) also includes a page of Prayer Goals. The goals include a section to list your Prayer Intentions, a Goals Checklist, and a place to list your weekly Acts of Love and Sacrifice:

- **Prayer Intentions**: This is an opportunity to give your worries away to God. Imagine taking these intentions from your heart and placing them in Jesus' outstretched hands. Pray especially for those people who stress you or have hurt you or a loved one. This is an amazing way to break the chains that bind you to hurt.
- **Goals Checklist**: We provide some helpful prayer and actions to help you grow in the practice of your faith.
- **Small Things with Great Love**: Here is a place to list the times that you did a small act for another person with great love. When you do the dishes when it's not really your responsibility, when you apologize when it's not your fault, when you forgive the rude person at the grocery store – write it down here.

Lastly, be assured of our prayers for you, and maybe one day we will meet in Heaven ... where there's no such thing as fear and anxiety.

For the great glory of God!

Sara & Scott Smith

Week One

first, Breathe

> Breathe in ...
> 7 seconds.
> Hold your breath ...
> 7 seconds.
> Breathe out ...
> 7 seconds.
> *Repeat.*
> As many times as you like.

second, Become aware of God's Presence

third, Thanksgiving

Lord, I realize that all, even myself, is a gift from you. Today, for what things am I most grateful?

fourth, Reflect

Jesus came and stood among them and said to them, "Peace be with you." When he had said this, he showed them his hands and his side. Then the disciples were glad when they saw the Lord. Jesus said to them again, "Peace be with you. As the Father has sent me, even so I send you."
John 20:19-21

fifth, Examination

Lord, open my eyes and ears to be more honest with myself. Show me what has been happening to me and in me this day. Today, how have I experienced your love?

sixth, Contrition

Today, what choices have been inadequate responses to your love?

seventh, Hope

Lord, let me look with longing toward the future. How will I let you lead me to a brighter tomorrow?

Weekly Prayer

"Take and Receive" Prayer

Take, Lord, and receive all my liberty,
My memory, my understanding,
And my entire will –
All that I have and call my own.
You have given it all to me.
To you, Lord, I return it.
Everything is yours;
Do with it what you will.
Give me only your love and your grace.
That is enough for me.
Amen.

Prayer Goals

Prayer Intentions

For whom or what do you want to pray this week? In particular, consider praying for those who frustrate or anger you, maybe even those who have harmed you or your loved ones.

_____
_____
_____
_____
_____
_____
_____
_____

> As St. (Mother) Teresa said, "Not all of us can do great things. But we can do ... *small things with great love*"

List your "small things" below:

_____
_____
_____
_____
_____
_____
_____
_____

Goals Checklist

Don't feel like you need to check all these boxes every week. Start with a goal of perhaps 2 or 3 and build from there.

- ☐ Spiritual Reading
- ☐ Share your faith with someone
- ☐ Attend Church Services
- ☐ Pray with somebody
- ☐ Volunteer at Homeless Shelter or Food Bank
- ☐ Attend a Bible Study

Week Two

first, Breathe

Breathe in ...
7 seconds.
Hold your breath ...
7 seconds.
Breathe out ...
7 seconds.

Repeat.

As many times as you like.

second, Become aware of God's Presence

third, Thanksgiving

Lord, I realize that all, even myself, is a gift from you. Today, for what things am I most grateful?

fourth, Reflect

"The past to mercy, the present to grace, the future to Providence ... Let us ask for grace ... each morning grace permits us ... to make it again to the evening."
— Chiara Corbella Petrillo, *A Witness to Joy*

fifth, Examination

Lord, open my eyes and ears to be more honest with myself. Show me what has been happening to me and in me this day. Today, how have I experienced your love?

sixth, Contrition

Today, what choices have been inadequate responses to your love?

seventh, Hope

Lord, let me look with longing toward the future. How will I let you lead me to a brighter tomorrow?

Weekly Prayer

Act of Hope

My God, relying on your
infinite goodness and promises,
I hope to obtain pardon of my sins,
Help of your grace,
And life everlasting
Through the merits of Jesus Christ,
My Lord and Redeemer
Amen.

Prayer Goals

Prayer Intentions

For whom or what do you want to pray this week? In particular, consider praying for those who frustrate or anger you, maybe even those who have harmed you or your loved ones.

_____
_____
_____
_____
_____
_____
_____
_____

> As St. (Mother) Teresa said, "Not all of us can do great things. But we can do ... *small things with great love*"

List your "small things" below:

_____
_____
_____
_____
_____
_____
_____
_____
_____

Goals Checklist

Don't feel like you need to check all these boxes every week. Start with a goal of perhaps 2 or 3 and build from there.

- ☐ Spiritual Reading
- ☐ Share your faith with someone
- ☐ Attend Church Services
- ☐ Pray with somebody
- ☐ Volunteer at Homeless Shelter or Food Bank
- ☐ Attend a Bible Study

Week Three

first, Breathe

Breathe in ...
7 seconds.
Hold your breath ...
7 seconds.
Breathe out ...
7 seconds.

Repeat.

As many times as you like.

second, Become aware of God's Presence

third, Thanksgiving

Lord, I realize that all, even myself, is a gift from you. Today, for what things am I most grateful?

fourth, Reflect

> There is no fear in love, but perfect love casts out fear. For fear has to do with punishment, and he who fears is not perfected in love.
> 1 John 4:18

fifth, Examination

Lord, open my eyes and ears to be more honest with myself. Show me what has been happening to me and in me this day. Today, how have I experienced your love?

sixth, Contrition

Today, what choices have been inadequate responses to your love?

seventh, Hope

Lord, let me look with longing toward the future. How will I let you lead me to a brighter tomorrow?

Weekly Prayer

Serenity Prayer

God, grant me the serenity
to accept the things I cannot change,
the courage to change the things I can,
and the wisdom to know the difference.
Living one day at a time,
enjoying one moment at a time;
accepting hardship as a pathway to peace;
taking, as Jesus did,
this sinful world as it is,
not as I would have it;
trusting that You will make all things right
if I surrender to Your will;
so that I may be reasonably happy in this life
and supremely happy with You
forever in the next.
Amen.

Prayer Goals

Prayer Intentions

For whom or what do you want to pray this week? In particular, consider praying for those who frustrate or anger you, maybe even those who have harmed you or your loved ones.

As St. (Mother) Teresa said, "Not all of us can do great things. But we can do ... *small things with great love*"

List your "small things" below:

Goals Checklist

Don't feel like you need to check all these boxes every week. Start with a goal of perhaps 2 or 3 and build from there.

- ☐ Spiritual Reading
- ☐ Share your faith with someone
- ☐ Attend Church Services
- ☐ Pray with somebody
- ☐ Volunteer at Homeless Shelter or Food Bank
- ☐ Attend a Bible Study

Week Four

first, Breathe

Breathe in ...
7 seconds.
Hold your breath ...
7 seconds.
Breathe out ...
7 seconds.

Repeat.

As many times as you like.

second, Become aware of God's Presence

third, Thanksgiving

Lord, I realize that all, even myself, is a gift from you. Today, for what things am I most grateful?

fourth, Reflect

Be strong and of good courage, do not fear or be in dread of them: for it is the Lord your God who goes with you; He will not fail you or forsake you.
Deuteronomy 31:6

fifth, Examination

Lord, open my eyes and ears to be more honest with myself. Show me what has been happening to me and in me this day. Today, how have I experienced your love?

sixth, Contrition

Today, what choices have been inadequate responses to your love?

seventh, Hope

Lord, let me look with longing toward the future. How will I let you lead me to a brighter tomorrow?

Weekly Prayer

Litany of Humility

O Jesus, meek and humble of heart, *Hear me.*
From the desire of being esteemed, *Deliver me, O Jesus.*
From the desire of being loved, *Deliver me, O Jesus.*
From the desire of being extolled, *Deliver me, O Jesus.*
From the desire of being honored, *Deliver me, O Jesus.*
From the desire of being praised, *Deliver me, O Jesus.*
From the desire of being preferred to others, *Deliver me, O Jesus.*
From the desire of being consulted, *Deliver me, O Jesus.*
From the desire of being approved, *Deliver me, O Jesus.*
From the fear of being humiliated, *Deliver me, O Jesus.*
From the fear of being despised, *Deliver me, O Jesus.*
From the fear of suffering rebukes, *Deliver me, O Jesus.*
From the fear of being calumniated, *Deliver me, O Jesus.*
From the fear of being forgotten, *Deliver me, O Jesus.*
From the fear of being ridiculed, *Deliver me, O Jesus.*
From the fear of being wronged, *Deliver me, O Jesus.*
From the fear of being suspected, *Deliver me, O Jesus.*
That others may be loved more than I,
Jesus, grant me the grace to desire it.
That others may be esteemed more than I,
Jesus, grant me the grace to desire it.
That, in the opinion of the world, others may increase and I may decrease,
Jesus, grant me the grace to desire it.
That others may be chosen and I set aside,
Jesus, grant me the grace to desire it.
That others may be praised and I go unnoticed,
Jesus, grant me the grace to desire it.
That others may be preferred to me in everything,
Jesus, grant me the grace to desire it.
That others may become holier than I, provided that I may become as holy as I should, *Jesus, grant me the grace to desire it.*
Amen.

Prayer Goals

Prayer Intentions

For whom or what do you want to pray this week? In particular, consider praying for those who frustrate or anger you, maybe even those who have harmed you or your loved ones.

_____
_____
_____
_____
_____
_____
_____
_____

As St. (Mother) Teresa said, "Not all of us can do great things. But we can do ... *small things with great love*"

List your "small things" below:

_____
_____
_____
_____
_____
_____
_____
_____
_____
_____

Goals Checklist

Don't feel like you need to check all these boxes every week. Start with a goal of perhaps 2 or 3 and build from there.

- ☐ Spiritual Reading
- ☐ Share your faith with someone
- ☐ Attend Church Services
- ☐ Pray with somebody
- ☐ Volunteer at Homeless Shelter or Food Bank
- ☐ Attend a Bible Study

Week Five

first, Breathe

Breathe in ...
7 seconds.
Hold your breath ...
7 seconds.
Breathe out ...
7 seconds.

Repeat.

As many times as you like.

second, Become aware of God's Presence

third, Thanksgiving

Lord, I realize that all, even myself, is a gift from you. Today, for what things am I most grateful?

fourth, Reflect

> But the Lord answered her, "Martha, Martha, you are anxious and troubled about many things; one thing is needful. Mary has chosen the good portion, which shall not be taken away from her."
> – Luke 10:41-42

fifth, Examination

Lord, open my eyes and ears to be more honest with myself. Show me what has been happening to me and in me this day. Today, how have I experienced your love?

sixth, Contrition

Today, what choices have been inadequate responses to your love?

seventh, Hope

Lord, let me look with longing toward the future. How will I let you lead me to a brighter tomorrow?

Weekly Prayer

Prayer for Calm

My Lord and my God,
I do not know what will happen to me today,
But what I do know is that
Nothing will happen to me today
That You and I together cannot handle.
This thought is enough
To bring me to face the day in peace.
I adore you in your wisdom and love.
I commend myself into your hands with the complete trust.
Amen.

Prayer Goals

Prayer Intentions

For whom or what do you want to pray this week? In particular, consider praying for those who frustrate or anger you, maybe even those who have harmed you or your loved ones.

_____
_____
_____
_____
_____
_____
_____
_____
_____

_____
_____
_____

> As St. (Mother) Teresa said, "Not all of us can do great things. But we can do ... *small things with great love*"

List your "small things" below:

_____
_____
_____
_____
_____
_____
_____
_____
_____
_____
_____
_____

Goals Checklist

Don't feel like you need to check all these boxes every week. Start with a goal of perhaps 2 or 3 and build from there.

- ☐ Spiritual Reading
- ☐ Share your faith with someone
- ☐ Attend Church Services
- ☐ Pray with somebody
- ☐ Volunteer at Homeless Shelter or Food Bank
- ☐ Attend a Bible Study

Week Six

first, Breathe

Breathe in ...
7 seconds.
Hold your breath ...
7 seconds.
Breathe out ...
7 seconds.

Repeat.

As many times as you like.

second, Become aware of God's Presence

third, Thanksgiving

Lord, I realize that all, even myself, is a gift from you. Today, for what things am I most grateful?

fourth, Reflect

*Anxiety in a man's heart weighs him down,
but a good word makes him glad.
Proverbs 12:25*

fifth, Examination

Lord, open my eyes and ears to be more honest with myself. Show me what has been happening to me and in me this day. Today, how have I experienced your love?

sixth, Contrition

Today, what choices have been inadequate responses to your love?

seventh, Hope

Lord, let me look with longing toward the future. How will I let you lead me to a brighter tomorrow?

Weekly Prayer

Litany of Trust, Part One
From the Sisters of Life

From the belief that I have to earn Your love,
Deliver me, Jesus.
From the fear that I am unlovable,
Deliver me, Jesus.
From the false security that I have what it takes,
Deliver me, Jesus.
From the fear that trusting You will leave me more destitute,
Deliver me, Jesus.
From all suspicion of Your words and promises,
Deliver me, Jesus.
From the rebellion against childlike dependency on You,
Deliver me, Jesus.
From refusals and reluctances in accepting Your will,
Deliver me, Jesus.
From anxiety about the future,
Deliver me, Jesus.
From resentment or excessive preoccupation with the past,
Deliver me, Jesus.
From restless self-seeking in the present moment,
Deliver me, Jesus.
From disbelief in Your love and presence,
Deliver me, Jesus.
From the fear of being asked to give more than I have,
Deliver me, Jesus.
From the belief that my life has no meaning or worth,
Deliver me, Jesus.
From the fear of what love demands,
Deliver me, Jesus.
From discouragement,
Deliver me, Jesus.

Prayer Goals

Prayer Intentions

For whom or what do you want to pray this week? In particular, consider praying for those who frustrate or anger you, maybe even those who have harmed you or your loved ones.

> As St. (Mother) Teresa said, "Not all of us can do great things. But we can do … *small things with great love*"

List your "small things" below:

Goals Checklist

Don't feel like you need to check all these boxes every week. Start with a goal of perhaps 2 or 3 and build from there.

- ☐ Spiritual Reading
- ☐ Share your faith with someone
- ☐ Attend Church Services
- ☐ Pray with somebody
- ☐ Volunteer at Homeless Shelter or Food Bank
- ☐ Attend a Bible Study

Week Seven

first, Breathe

Breathe in ...
7 seconds.
Hold your breath ...
7 seconds.
Breathe out ...
7 seconds.

Repeat.

As many times as you like.

second, Become aware of God's Presence

third, Thanksgiving

Lord, I realize that all, even myself, is a gift from you. Today, for what things am I most grateful?

fourth, Reflect

Have I not commanded you? Be strong and of good courage; be not frightened, neither be dismayed; for the Lord your God is with you wherever you go.
Joshua 1:9

fifth, Examination

Lord, open my eyes and ears to be more honest with myself. Show me what has been happening to me and in me this day. Today, how have I experienced your love?

_____
_____
_____
_____
_____
_____
_____
_____

sixth, Contrition

Today, what choices have been inadequate responses to your love?

_____
_____
_____
_____
_____
_____

seventh, Hope

Lord, let me look with longing toward the future. How will I let you lead me to a brighter tomorrow?

_____
_____
_____
_____
_____
_____

Weekly Prayer

Litany of Trust, Part Two
From the Sisters of Life

That You are continually holding me, sustaining me, loving me, *Jesus, I trust in You.*
That Your love goes deeper than my sins and failings and transforms me, *Jesus, I trust in You.*
That not knowing what tomorrow brings is an invitation to lean on You, *Jesus, I trust in You.*
That You are with me in my suffering, *Jesus, I trust in You.*
That my suffering, united to Your own, will bear fruit in this life and the next, *Jesus, I trust in You.*
That You will not leave me orphan, that You are present in Your Church, *Jesus, I trust in You.*
That Your plan is better than anything else, *Jesus, I trust in You.*
That You always hear me and in Your goodness always respond to me *Jesus, I trust in You.*
That You give me the grace to accept forgiveness and to forgive others *Jesus, I trust in You.*
That You give me all the strength I need for what is asked *Jesus, I trust in You.*
That my life is a gift, *Jesus, I trust in You.*
That You will teach me to trust You, *Jesus, I trust in You.*
That You are my Lord and my God, *Jesus, I trust in You.*
That I am Your beloved one, *Jesus, I trust in You.*

Prayer Goals

Prayer Intentions

For whom or what do you want to pray this week? In particular, consider praying for those who frustrate or anger you, maybe even those who have harmed you or your loved ones.

> As St. (Mother) Teresa said, "Not all of us can do great things. But we can do ... *small things with great love*"

List your "small things" below:

Goals Checklist

Don't feel like you need to check all these boxes every week. Start with a goal of perhaps 2 or 3 and build from there.

- [ ] Spiritual Reading
- [ ] Share your faith with someone
- [ ] Attend Church Services
- [ ] Pray with somebody
- [ ] Volunteer at Homeless Shelter or Food Bank
- [ ] Attend a Bible Study

Week Eight

first, Breathe

Breathe in …
7 seconds.
Hold your breath …
7 seconds.
Breathe out …
7 seconds.

Repeat.

As many times as you like.

second, Become aware of God's Presence

third, Thanksgiving

Lord, I realize that all, even myself, is a gift from you. Today, for what things am I most grateful?

fourth, Reflect

When I am afraid, I put my trust in thee.
In God, whose word I praise, in God I trust without a fear.
What can flesh do to me?
Psalm 56:3-4

fifth, Examination

Lord, open my eyes and ears to be more honest with myself. Show me what has been happening to me and in me this day. Today, how have I experienced your love?

sixth, Contrition

Today, what choices have been inadequate responses to your love?

seventh, Hope

Lord, let me look with longing toward the future. How will I let you lead me to a brighter tomorrow?

Weekly Prayer

Prayer for Peace and Calm
From John Greenleaf Whittier

Dear Lord and Father of humankind,
Forgive our foolish ways;
Reclothe us in our rightful mind,
In purer lives Thy service find,
In deeper reverence, praise.

Drop Thy still dews of quietness,
Till all our strivings cease;
Take from our souls the strain and stress,
And let our ordered lives confess
The beauty of Thy peace.

Breathe through the heats of our desire
Thy coolness and Thy balm;
Let sense be dumb, let flesh retire;
Speak through the earthquake, wind, and fire,
O still, small voice of calm.

Prayer Goals

Prayer Intentions

For whom or what do you want to pray this week? In particular, consider praying for those who frustrate or anger you, maybe even those who have harmed you or your loved ones.

_____
_____
_____
_____
_____
_____
_____
_____

> As St. (Mother) Teresa said, "Not all of us can do great things. But we can do ... *small things with great love*"

List your "small things" below:

_____
_____
_____
_____
_____
_____
_____
_____
_____
_____

Goals Checklist

Don't feel like you need to check all these boxes every week. Start with a goal of perhaps 2 or 3 and build from there.

- [ ] Spiritual Reading
- [ ] Share your faith with someone
- [ ] Attend Church Services
- [ ] Pray with somebody
- [ ] Volunteer at Homeless Shelter or Food Bank
- [ ] Attend a Bible Study

Week Nine

first, Breathe

Breathe in ...
7 seconds.
Hold your breath ...
7 seconds.
Breathe out ...
7 seconds.

Repeat.

As many times as you like.

second, Become aware of God's Presence

third, Thanksgiving

Lord, I realize that all, even myself, is a gift from you. Today, for what things am I most grateful?

fourth, Reflect

In peace I will lie down and sleep;
for Thou alone, O Lord, makest me dwell in safety.
- Psalm 4:8

fifth, Examination

Lord, open my eyes and ears to be more honest with myself. Show me what has been happening to me and in me this day. Today, how have I experienced your love?

sixth, Contrition

Today, what choices have been inadequate responses to your love?

seventh, Hope

Lord, let me look with longing toward the future. How will I let you lead me to a brighter tomorrow?

Weekly Prayer

A Prayer for Soothing Panic Attacks

Dear God,
I come before You to
Lay my panic and anxiety at Your feet.
When I'm crushed by my fears and worries,
remind me of Your power and Your grace.
Fill me with Your peace
As I trust in You and You alone.
I know I can't beat this on my own,
but I also know that I have You, Lord,
And You have already paid the ultimate price
To carry my burdens.
For this I thank you.
Amen.

Prayer Goals

Prayer Intentions

For whom or what do you want to pray this week? In particular, consider praying for those who frustrate or anger you, maybe even those who have harmed you or your loved ones.

As St. (Mother) Teresa said, "Not all of us can do great things. But we can do ... *small things with great love*"

List your "small things" below:

Goals Checklist

Don't feel like you need to check all these boxes every week. Start with a goal of perhaps 2 or 3 and build from there.

- [ ] Spiritual Reading
- [ ] Share your faith with someone
- [ ] Attend Church Services
- [ ] Pray with somebody
- [ ] Volunteer at Homeless Shelter or Food Bank
- [ ] Attend a Bible Study

Week Ten

first, Breathe

Breathe in ...
7 seconds.
Hold your breath ...
7 seconds.
Breathe out ...
7 seconds.

Repeat.

As many times as you like.

second, Become aware of God's Presence

third, Thanksgiving

Lord, I realize that all, even myself, is a gift from you. Today, for what things am I most grateful?

fourth,
Reflect

O Israel, trust in the Lord! He is their help and their shield.
O house of Aaron, put your trust in the Lord! He is their help and their shield.
You who fear the Lord, trust in the Lord! He is their help and their shield.
Psalm 115:9-11

fifth, Examination

Lord, open my eyes and ears to be more honest with myself. Show me what has been happening to me and in me this day. Today, how have I experienced your love?

sixth, Contrition

Today, what choices have been inadequate responses to your love?

seventh, Hope

Lord, let me look with longing toward the future. How will I let you lead me to a brighter tomorrow?

Weekly Prayer

Your Peace

God,
Who is more than we can ever comprehend,
Help us to seek You,
And You alone.
Help us to stand before all that we could do
And seek what You would do,
And do that.
Lift from us our need
To achieve all that we can be
And instead,
Surrender to what You can be in us.
Give us ways to refrain from the busyness
That will put us on edge and off center,
Give us today Your peace.
Amen.

Prayer Goals

Prayer Intentions

For whom or what do you want to pray this week? In particular, consider praying for those who frustrate or anger you, maybe even those who have harmed you or your loved ones.

As St. (Mother) Teresa said, "Not all of us can do great things. But we can do ... *small things with great love*"

List your "small things" below:

Goals Checklist

Don't feel like you need to check all these boxes every week. Start with a goal of perhaps 2 or 3 and build from there.

- ☐ Spiritual Reading
- ☐ Share your faith with someone
- ☐ Attend Church Services
- ☐ Pray with somebody
- ☐ Volunteer at Homeless Shelter or Food Bank
- ☐ Attend a Bible Study

Week Eleven

first, Breathe

Breathe in ...
7 seconds.
Hold your breath ...
7 seconds.
Breathe out ...
7 seconds.

Repeat.

As many times as you like.

second, Become aware of God's Presence

third, Thanksgiving

Lord, I realize that all, even myself, is a gift from you. Today, for what things am I most grateful?

fourth, Reflect

*"The Lord is my light and my salvation—whom shall I fear?
The Lord is the stronghold of my life—of whom shall I be afraid?"*
Psalm 27:3

fifth, Examination

Lord, open my eyes and ears to be more honest with myself. Show me what has been happening to me and in me this day. Today, how have I experienced your love?

sixth, Contrition

Today, what choices have been inadequate responses to your love?

seventh, Hope

Lord, let me look with longing toward the future. How will I let you lead me to a brighter tomorrow?

Weekly Prayer

Prayer for Strength
From Psalm 27:1b

Dear Jesus,
You are the strength of my life;
You are my rock, my fortress and my protector;
Therefore, whom shall I be afraid?
You are my shield,
My strong-tower and my stronghold.
I will call to You because
You are worthy to be praised.
So, Father,
I thank you for being my strength
And My God in whom I trust.
Amen.

Prayer Goals

Prayer Intentions

For whom or what do you want to pray this week? In particular, consider praying for those who frustrate or anger you, maybe even those who have harmed you or your loved ones.

As St. (Mother) Teresa said, "Not all of us can do great things. But we can do ... *small things with great love*"

List your "small things" below:

Goals Checklist

Don't feel like you need to check all these boxes every week. Start with a goal of perhaps 2 or 3 and build from there.

- [ ] Spiritual Reading
- [ ] Share your faith with someone
- [ ] Attend Church Services
- [ ] Pray with somebody
- [ ] Volunteer at Homeless Shelter or Food Bank
- [ ] Attend a Bible Study

Week Twelve

first, Breathe

Breathe in ... 7 seconds.
Hold your breath ... 7 seconds.
Breathe out ... 7 seconds.

Repeat.

As many times as you like.

second, Become aware of God's Presence

third, Thanksgiving

Lord, I realize that all, even myself, is a gift from you. Today, for what things am I most grateful?

fourth, Reflect

"Therefore do not be anxious about tomorrow,
For tomorrow will be anxious for itself.
Let the day's own trouble be sufficient for the day."
Matthew 6:34

fifth, Examination

Lord, open my eyes and ears to be more honest with myself. Show me what has been happening to me and in me this day. Today, how have I experienced your love?

sixth, Contrition

Today, what choices have been inadequate responses to your love?

seventh, Hope

Lord, let me look with longing toward the future. How will I let you lead me to a brighter tomorrow?

Weekly Prayer

Prayer of St. Francis

Lord, make me an instrument of your peace:
where there is hatred, let me sow love;
where there is injury, pardon;
where there is doubt, faith;
where there is despair, hope;
where there is darkness, light;
where there is sadness, joy.

O divine Master, grant that I may not so much seek
to be consoled as to console,
to be understood as to understand,
to be loved as to love.
For it is in giving that we receive,
it is in pardoning that we are pardoned,
and it is in dying that we are born to eternal life.
Amen.

Prayer Goals

Prayer Intentions

For whom or what do you want to pray this week? In particular, consider praying for those who frustrate or anger you, maybe even those who have harmed you or your loved ones.

_____
_____
_____
_____
_____
_____
_____
_____
_____

> As St. (Mother) Teresa said, "Not all of us can do great things. But we can do ... *small things with great love*"

List your "small things" below:

_____
_____
_____
_____
_____
_____
_____
_____
_____
_____

Goals Checklist

Don't feel like you need to check all these boxes every week. Start with a goal of perhaps 2 or 3 and build from there.

- [ ] Spiritual Reading
- [ ] Share your faith with someone
- [ ] Attend Church Services
- [ ] Pray with somebody
- [ ] Volunteer at Homeless Shelter or Food Bank
- [ ] Attend a Bible Study

Week Thirteen

first, Breathe

Breathe in ...
7 seconds.
Hold your breath ...
7 seconds.
Breathe out ...
7 seconds.

Repeat.

As many times as you like.

second, Become aware of God's Presence

third, Thanksgiving

Lord, I realize that all, even myself, is a gift from you. Today, for what things am I most grateful?

fourth, Reflect

Cast all your anxieties on Him, for He cares about you.
1 Peter 5:7

fifth, Examination

Lord, open my eyes and ears to be more honest with myself. Show me what has been happening to me and in me this day. Today, how have I experienced your love?

_____
_____
_____
_____
_____
_____
_____

sixth, Contrition

Today, what choices have been inadequate responses to your love?

_____
_____
_____
_____
_____

seventh, Hope

Lord, let me look with longing toward the future. How will I let you lead me to a brighter tomorrow?

_____
_____
_____
_____
_____

Weekly Prayer

I Want To Be Available

Holy and perfect God,
You know I want to be available.
Help that desire sink deeply enough
Into my being
For me to actually change
And to say "no" to a least one worthy,
But not urgent, task today.
Give me the ability to be open
To the life I am leading;
Not the one I am planning to lead.

Prayer Goals

Prayer Intentions

For whom or what do you want to pray this week? In particular, consider praying for those who frustrate or anger you, maybe even those who have harmed you or your loved ones.

As St. (Mother) Teresa said, "Not all of us can do great things. But we can do ... *small things with great love*"

List your "small things" below:

Goals Checklist

Don't feel like you need to check all these boxes every week. Start with a goal of perhaps 2 or 3 and build from there.

- [ ] Spiritual Reading
- [ ] Share your faith with someone
- [ ] Attend Church Services
- [ ] Pray with somebody
- [ ] Volunteer at Homeless Shelter or Food Bank
- [ ] Attend a Bible Study

Week Fourteen

first, Breathe

Breathe in ...
7 seconds.
Hold your breath ...
7 seconds.
Breathe out ...
7 seconds.

Repeat.

As many times as you like.

second, Become aware of God's Presence

third, Thanksgiving

Lord, I realize that all, even myself, is a gift from you. Today, for what things am I most grateful?

fourth, Reflect

> For I, the Lord your God, hold your right hand;
> it is I who say to you, "Fear not, I will help you."
> Isaiah 41:13

fifth, Examination

Lord, open my eyes and ears to be more honest with myself. Show me what has been happening to me and in me this day. Today, how have I experienced your love?

_____
_____
_____
_____
_____
_____
_____

sixth, Contrition

Today, what choices have been inadequate responses to your love?

_____
_____
_____
_____
_____

seventh, Hope

Lord, let me look with longing toward the future. How will I let you lead me to a brighter tomorrow?

_____
_____
_____
_____
_____

Weekly *Prayer*

A Prayer for Calming a Troubled Heart

Loving God,
Please grant me peace of mind
And calm my troubled heart.
My soul is like a turbulent sea.
I can't seem to find my balance,
So I stumble and worry constantly.

Give me the strength and clarity of mind
To find my purpose and walk the path
You've laid out for me.
I trust Your Love, God,
And know that You will heal this stress.
Just as the sun rises each day
Against the dark of night.
Please bring me clarity with the light of God.
In Your Name I pray.
Amen.

Prayer Goals

Prayer Intentions

For whom or what do you want to pray this week? In particular, consider praying for those who frustrate or anger you, maybe even those who have harmed you or your loved ones.

_____
_____
_____
_____
_____
_____

> As St. (Mother) Teresa said, "Not all of us can do great things. But we can do ... *small things with great love*"

List your "small things" below:

_____
_____
_____
_____
_____
_____
_____
_____
_____
_____

Goals Checklist

Don't feel like you need to check all these boxes every week. Start with a goal of perhaps 2 or 3 and build from there.

- ☐ Spiritual Reading
- ☐ Share your faith with someone
- ☐ Attend Church Services
- ☐ Pray with somebody
- ☐ Volunteer at Homeless Shelter or Food Bank
- ☐ Attend a Bible Study

Week Fifteen

first, Breathe

Breathe in ...
7 seconds.
Hold your breath ...
7 seconds.
Breathe out ...
7 seconds.

Repeat.

As many times as you like.

second, Become aware of God's Presence

third, Thanksgiving

Lord, I realize that all, even myself, is a gift from you. Today, for what things am I most grateful?

fourth, Reflect

For you did not receive the spirit of slavery to fall back into fear, but you have received the spirit of sonship. When we cry, "Abba! Father!" it is the Spirit himself bearing witness with our spirit that we are children of God, and if children, then heirs, heirs of God and fellow heirs with Christ, provided we suffer with him in order that we may also be glorified with him.
Romans 8:15

fifth, Examination

Lord, open my eyes and ears to be more honest with myself. Show me what has been happening to me and in me this day. Today, how have I experienced your love?

_____
_____
_____
_____
_____
_____
_____

sixth, Contrition

Today, what choices have been inadequate responses to your love?

seventh, Hope

Lord, let me look with longing toward the future. How will I let you lead me to a brighter tomorrow?

Weekly Prayer

A Prayer for Christ's Peace

Lord, please put Your peace in my heart.
I'm worried and anxious.
My mind races and obsesses.
I can't help thinking about my problems.
And the more I think about them,
The more depressed I become.
I feel like I'm sinking down in quicksand
And can't get out.
Calm me, Lord.
Slow me down,
Put Your peace in my heart.

No matter what problem I have, Lord,
You are bigger,
You are more powerful than it is.
So I bring my problem to You.
I know what I want.
I know my will, but I do not know Yours.
I do not know how You will use this problem for my salvation.
I do not know what good You will work from this evil.
But I trust You.
I trust Your goodness and Your wisdom.
So I place myself in Your hands.
Please fill my heart with peace.
Amen.

Prayer Goals

Prayer Intentions

For whom or what do you want to pray this week? In particular, consider praying for those who frustrate or anger you, maybe even those who have harmed you or your loved ones.

_____
_____
_____
_____
_____
_____
_____
_____

> As St. (Mother) Teresa said, "Not all of us can do great things. But we can do … *small things with great love*"

List your "small things" below:

_____
_____
_____
_____
_____
_____
_____
_____
_____
_____
_____
_____

Goals Checklist

Don't feel like you need to check all these boxes every week. Start with a goal of perhaps 2 or 3 and build from there.

- ☐ Spiritual Reading
- ☐ Share your faith with someone
- ☐ Attend Church Services
- ☐ Pray with somebody
- ☐ Volunteer at Homeless Shelter or Food Bank
- ☐ Attend a Bible Study

Week Sixteen

first, Breathe

Breathe in ...
7 seconds.
Hold your breath ...
7 seconds.
Breathe out ...
7 seconds.

Repeat.

As many times as you like.

second, Become aware of God's Presence

third, Thanksgiving

Lord, I realize that all, even myself, is a gift from you. Today, for what things am I most grateful?

fourth, Reflect

But they who wait for the Lord shall renew their strength,
they shall mount up with wings like eagles,
they shall run and not be weary, they shall walk and not faint.
Isaiah 40:31

fifth, Examination

Lord, open my eyes and ears to be more honest with myself. Show me what has been happening to me and in me this day. Today, how have I experienced your love?

sixth, Contrition

Today, what choices have been inadequate responses to your love?

seventh, Hope

Lord, let me look with longing toward the future. How will I let you lead me to a brighter tomorrow?

Weekly Prayer

Anima Christi

Soul of Christ, *sanctify me.*
Body of Christ, *save me.*
Blood of Christ, *inebriate me.*
Water from the side of Christ, *wash me.*
Passion of Christ, *strengthen me.*
O Good Jesus, *hear me.*
Within your wounds, *hide me.*
Permit me not to be separated from you.
From the wicked foe, *defend me.*
At the hour of my death, *call me*
And bid me come to you,
That with your saints I may praise you
Forever and ever.
Amen.

Prayer Goals

Prayer Intentions

For whom or what do you want to pray this week? In particular, consider praying for those who frustrate or anger you, maybe even those who have harmed you or your loved ones.

_____
_____
_____
_____
_____
_____
_____
_____

As St. (Mother) Teresa said, "Not all of us can do great things. But we can do ... *small things with great love*"

List your "small things" below:

_____
_____
_____
_____
_____
_____
_____
_____
_____
_____
_____
_____

Goals Checklist

Don't feel like you need to check all these boxes every week. Start with a goal of perhaps 2 or 3 and build from there.

- [ ] Spiritual Reading
- [ ] Share your faith with someone
- [ ] Attend Church Services
- [ ] Pray with somebody
- [ ] Volunteer at Homeless Shelter or Food Bank
- [ ] Attend a Bible Study

Week Seventeen

first, Breathe

Breathe in ...
7 seconds.
Hold your breath ...
7 seconds.
Breathe out ...
7 seconds.

Repeat.

As many times as you like.

second, Become aware of God's Presence

third, Thanksgiving

Lord, I realize that all, even myself, is a gift from you. Today, for what things am I most grateful?

fourth, Reflect

"He got up, rebuked the wind and said to the waves, "Quiet! Be still!" Then the wind died down and it was completely calm. He said to his disciples, "Why are you so afraid? Do you still have no faith?"
Mark 4:39-40

fifth, Examination

Lord, open my eyes and ears to be more honest with myself. Show me what has been happening to me and in me this day. Today, how have I experienced your love?

sixth, Contrition

Today, what choices have been inadequate responses to your love?

seventh, Hope

Lord, let me look with longing toward the future. How will I let you lead me to a brighter tomorrow?

Weekly Prayer

A Prayer for Hope

Dear Lord,
I am your humble servant and
I kneel before You today,
Helpless and weak.
I need Your hope for love,
Kindness and for a better life, Lord.
I ask that You fill me from head to toe
With Your everlasting light.
Bathe me in Your glory, Lord,
And show me that everything is
According to Your plan.
Help me walk in Your glorious light and
Show me the path,
So that I may follow You in faith.
Amen.

Prayer Goals

Prayer Intentions

For whom or what do you want to pray this week? In particular, consider praying for those who frustrate or anger you, maybe even those who have harmed you or your loved ones.

_____
_____
_____
_____
_____
_____
_____

As St. (Mother) Teresa said, "Not all of us can do great things. But we can do ... *small things with great love*"

List your "small things" below:

_____
_____
_____
_____
_____
_____
_____
_____
_____
_____
_____

Goals Checklist

Don't feel like you need to check all these boxes every week. Start with a goal of perhaps 2 or 3 and build from there.

- [ ] Spiritual Reading
- [ ] Share your faith with someone
- [ ] Attend Church Services
- [ ] Pray with somebody
- [ ] Volunteer at Homeless Shelter or Food Bank
- [ ] Attend a Bible Study

Week Eighteen

first, Breathe

Breathe in ... 7 seconds.
Hold your breath ... 7 seconds.
Breathe out ... 7 seconds.

Repeat.

As many times as you like.

second, Become aware of God's Presence

third, Thanksgiving

Lord, I realize that all, even myself, is a gift from you. Today, for what things am I most grateful?

fourth, Reflect

"But even if you suffer for doing what is right, God will reward you for it. So don't worry or be afraid of their threats."
1 Peter 3:14

fifth, Examination

Lord, open my eyes and ears to be more honest with myself. Show me what has been happening to me and in me this day. Today, how have I experienced your love?

sixth, Contrition

Today, what choices have been inadequate responses to your love?

seventh, Hope

Lord, let me look with longing toward the future. How will I let you lead me to a brighter tomorrow?

Weekly Prayer

A Prayer to Cast Out Fear

I know that worrying gets me nowhere.
Yet I still allow worry and anxiety to consume me.
In times such as these,
Lord Jesus,
I ask you to grant me
A great amount of strength, faith, and courage
To fight off the doubt and fear
Within my mind and heart.
Faith casts out fear
While fear casts out faith.

Prayer Goals

Prayer Intentions

For whom or what do you want to pray this week? In particular, consider praying for those who frustrate or anger you, maybe even those who have harmed you or your loved ones.

_____
_____
_____
_____
_____
_____
_____
_____

> As St. (Mother) Teresa said, "Not all of us can do great things. But we can do ...
> *small things with great love*"

List your "small things" below:

_____
_____
_____
_____
_____
_____
_____
_____
_____

Goals Checklist

Don't feel like you need to check all these boxes every week. Start with a goal of perhaps 2 or 3 and build from there.

- ☐ Spiritual Reading
- ☐ Share your faith with someone
- ☐ Attend Church Services
- ☐ Pray with somebody
- ☐ Volunteer at Homeless Shelter or Food Bank
- ☐ Attend a Bible Study

Week Nineteen

first, Breathe

Breathe in ...
7 seconds.
Hold your breath ...
7 seconds.
Breathe out ...
7 seconds.

Repeat.

As many times as you like.

second, Become aware of God's Presence

third, Thanksgiving

Lord, I realize that all, even myself, is a gift from you. Today, for what things am I most grateful?

fourth,
Reflect

> I sought the Lord, and he answered me, and delivered me from all my fears. Look to him, and be radiant; so your faces shall never be ashamed. This poor man cried, and the Lord heard him, and saved him out of all his troubles. The angel of the Lord encamps around those who fear him, and delivers them. O taste and see that the Lord is good! Happy is the man who takes refuge in him!
> Psalm 34:4-8

fifth, Examination

Lord, open my eyes and ears to be more honest with myself. Show me what has been happening to me and in me this day. Today, how have I experienced your love?

_____
_____
_____
_____
_____
_____
_____
_____

sixth Contrition

Today, what choices have been inadequate responses to your love?

_____
_____
_____
_____
_____
_____

seventh, Hope

Lord, let me look with longing toward the future. How will I let you lead me to a brighter tomorrow?

_____
_____
_____
_____
_____
_____

Weekly Prayer

A Prayer for the Weary

Father, my heart is heavy.
I feel like I have to carry the burden alone.
Words like overwhelmed, distraught, exhausted
Seem to describe where I am.
I am not sure how to let you carry my heavy
Load, so please show me how.
Take it from me.
Let me rest and be refreshed
So that my heart won't be
So heavy in the morning.
In Jesus' name.
Amen.

Prayer Goals

Prayer Intentions

For whom or what do you want to pray this week? In particular, consider praying for those who frustrate or anger you, maybe even those who have harmed you or your loved ones.

_____
_____
_____
_____
_____
_____
_____

As St. (Mother) Teresa said, "Not all of us can do great things. But we can do ... *small things with great love*"

List your "small things" below:

_____
_____
_____
_____
_____
_____
_____
_____
_____
_____

Goals Checklist

Don't feel like you need to check all these boxes every week. Start with a goal of perhaps 2 or 3 and build from there.

- ☐ Spiritual Reading
- ☐ Share your faith with someone
- ☐ Attend Church Services
- ☐ Pray with somebody
- ☐ Volunteer at Homeless Shelter or Food Bank
- ☐ Attend a Bible Study

Week Twenty

first, Breathe

Breathe in ... 7 seconds.
Hold your breath ... 7 seconds.
Breathe out ... 7 seconds.

Repeat.

As many times as you like.

second, Become aware of God's Presence

third, Thanksgiving

Lord, I realize that all, even myself, is a gift from you. Today, for what things am I most grateful?

fourth, Reflect

"And do not fear those who kill the body but cannot kill the soul; rather fear him who can destroy both soul and body in hell. Are not two sparrows sold for a penny? And not one of them will fall to the ground without your Father's will. But even the hairs of your head are all numbered. Fear not, therefore; you are of more value than many sparrows."
Matthew 10:28-31

fifth, Examination

Lord, open my eyes and ears to be more honest with myself. Show me what has been happening to me and in me this day. Today, how have I experienced your love?

sixth, Contrition

Today, what choices have been inadequate responses to your love?

seventh, Hope

Lord, let me look with longing toward the future. How will I let you lead me to a brighter tomorrow?

Weekly Prayer

A Prayer for Letting Go of Worries

Heavenly Father,
Lately I've been so worried about
Things that are out of my control.
Help me to trust that
You are working out
Every little detail of my life and
That I have nothing to fear
Or worry about.
In Jesus' name,
Amen.

Prayer Goals

Prayer Intentions

For whom or what do you want to pray this week? In particular, consider praying for those who frustrate or anger you, maybe even those who have harmed you or your loved ones.

_____
_____
_____
_____
_____
_____
_____

> As St. (Mother) Teresa said, "Not all of us can do great things. But we can do ... *small things with great love*"

List your "small things" below:

_____
_____
_____
_____
_____
_____
_____
_____
_____

Goals Checklist

Don't feel like you need to check all these boxes every week. Start with a goal of perhaps 2 or 3 and build from there.

- [ ] Spiritual Reading
- [ ] Share your faith with someone
- [ ] Attend Church Services
- [ ] Pray with somebody
- [ ] Volunteer at Homeless Shelter or Food Bank
- [ ] Attend a Bible Study

Week Twenty-One

first, Breathe

Breathe in …
7 seconds.
Hold your breath …
7 seconds.
Breathe out …
7 seconds.

Repeat.

As many times as you like.

second, Become aware of God's Presence

third, Thanksgiving

Lord, I realize that all, even myself, is a gift from you. Today, for what things am I most grateful?

fourth, Reflect

Fear not, for you will not be ashamed; be not confounded, for you will not be put to shame; for you will forget the shame of your youth, and the reproach of your widowhood you will remember no more. For your Maker is your husband, the Lord of hosts is his name; and the Holy One of Israel is your Redeemer, the God of the whole earth he is called.
Isaiah 54:4-5

fifth, Examination

Lord, open my eyes and ears to be more honest with myself. Show me what has been happening to me and in me this day. Today, how have I experienced your love?

sixth, Contrition

Today, what choices have been inadequate responses to your love?

seventh, Hope

Lord, let me look with longing toward the future. How will I let you lead me to a brighter tomorrow?

Weekly Prayer

Magnificat

My soul proclaims the greatness of the Lord,
My spirit rejoices in God my Savior;
For he has looked with favor on his lowly servant.
From this day all generations will call me blessed:
The Almighty has done great things for me,
And holy is his Name.
He has mercy on those who fear him
in every generation.
He has shown the strength of his arm,
He has scattered the proud in their conceit.
He has cast down the mighty from their thrones,
And has lifted up the lowly.
He has filled the hungry with good things,
And the rich he has sent away empty.
He has come to the help of his servant Israel
For he has remembered his promise of mercy,
The promise he made to our fathers,
To Abraham and his children forever.

Prayer Goals

Prayer Intentions

For whom or what do you want to pray this week? In particular, consider praying for those who frustrate or anger you, maybe even those who have harmed you or your loved ones.

_____
_____
_____
_____
_____
_____
_____
_____

As St. (Mother) Teresa said, "Not all of us can do great things. But we can do ... *small things with great love*"

List your "small things" below:

_____
_____
_____
_____
_____
_____
_____
_____
_____
_____
_____

Goals Checklist

Don't feel like you need to check all these boxes every week. Start with a goal of perhaps 2 or 3 and build from there.

- ☐ Spiritual Reading
- ☐ Share your faith with someone
- ☐ Attend Church Services
- ☐ Pray with somebody
- ☐ Volunteer at Homeless Shelter or Food Bank
- ☐ Attend a Bible Study

Week Twenty-Two

first, Breathe

Breathe in ...
7 seconds.
Hold your breath ...
7 seconds.
Breathe out ...
7 seconds.

Repeat.

As many times as you like.

second, Become aware of God's Presence

third, Thanksgiving

Lord, I realize that all, even myself, is a gift from you. Today, for what things am I most grateful?

fourth, Reflect

When the cares of my heart are many,
thy consolations cheer my soul.
Psalm 94:19

fifth, Examination

Lord, open my eyes and ears to be more honest with myself. Show me what has been happening to me and in me this day. Today, how have I experienced your love?

sixth, Contrition

Today, what choices have been inadequate responses to your love?

seventh, Hope

Lord, let me look with longing toward the future. How will I let you lead me to a brighter tomorrow?

Weekly Prayer

A Prayer for Unburdening the Mind

Dear Loving Lord,
I am feeling stress, I am worried.
Too many things occupy my mind.
Won't you help me?
Show me, Lord,
Your order and Your plans are eternal.
Let me trust in Your Will alone.
Your Word tells me where there is love,
there is no fear.
Let me be filled with Your Love.
The perfect love
That tells me I am not condemned,
but I am saved.
I can do all things through You.
You strengthen me.
In Jesus name,
Amen.

Prayer Goals

Prayer Intentions

For whom or what do you want to pray this week? In particular, consider praying for those who frustrate or anger you, maybe even those who have harmed you or your loved ones.

_____
_____
_____
_____
_____
_____
_____
_____
_____
_____

> As St. (Mother) Teresa said, "Not all of us can do great things. But we can do ... *small things with great love*"

List your "small things" below:

_____
_____
_____
_____
_____
_____
_____
_____
_____
_____
_____
_____

Goals Checklist

Don't feel like you need to check all these boxes every week. Start with a goal of perhaps 2 or 3 and build from there.

- ☐ Spiritual Reading
- ☐ Share your faith with someone
- ☐ Attend Church Services
- ☐ Pray with somebody
- ☐ Volunteer at Homeless Shelter or Food Bank
- ☐ Attend a Bible Study

Week Twenty-Three

first, Breathe

Breathe in ...
7 seconds.
Hold your breath ...
7 seconds.
Breathe out ...
7 seconds.

Repeat.

As many times as you like.

second, Become aware of God's Presence

third, Thanksgiving

Lord, I realize that all, even myself, is a gift from you. Today, for what things am I most grateful?

fourth, Reflect

> Do not be anxious about anything, but in every situation, by prayer and petition, with thanksgiving, present your requests to God. And the peace of God, which transcends all understanding, will guard your hearts and your minds in Christ Jesus.
> Philippians 4:6-7

fifth, Examination

Lord, open my eyes and ears to be more honest with myself. Show me what has been happening to me and in me this day. Today, how have I experienced your love?

_____
_____
_____
_____
_____
_____
_____
_____

sixth, Contrition

Today, what choices have been inadequate responses to your love?

_____
_____
_____
_____
_____
_____

seventh, Hope

Lord, let me look with longing toward the future. How will I let you lead me to a brighter tomorrow?

_____
_____
_____
_____
_____
_____

Weekly Prayer

St. Francis' Canticle of the Sun

Be praised, my Lord,
For all your creatures,
And first for brother sun,
Who makes the day bright and luminous.
He is beautiful and radiant
With great splendor
He is the image of You,
Most high.
Be praised, my Lord,
For sister moon and the stars.
You placed them in the sky,
So bright and twinkling.

Prayer Goals

Prayer Intentions

For whom or what do you want to pray this week? In particular, consider praying for those who frustrate or anger you, maybe even those who have harmed you or your loved ones.

_____
_____
_____
_____
_____
_____
_____

As St. (Mother) Teresa said, "Not all of us can do great things. But we can do ... *small things with great love*"

List your "small things" below:

_____
_____
_____
_____
_____
_____
_____
_____
_____
_____

Goals Checklist

Don't feel like you need to check all these boxes every week. Start with a goal of perhaps 2 or 3 and build from there.

- ☐ Spiritual Reading
- ☐ Share your faith with someone
- ☐ Attend Church Services
- ☐ Pray with somebody
- ☐ Volunteer at Homeless Shelter or Food Bank
- ☐ Attend a Bible Study

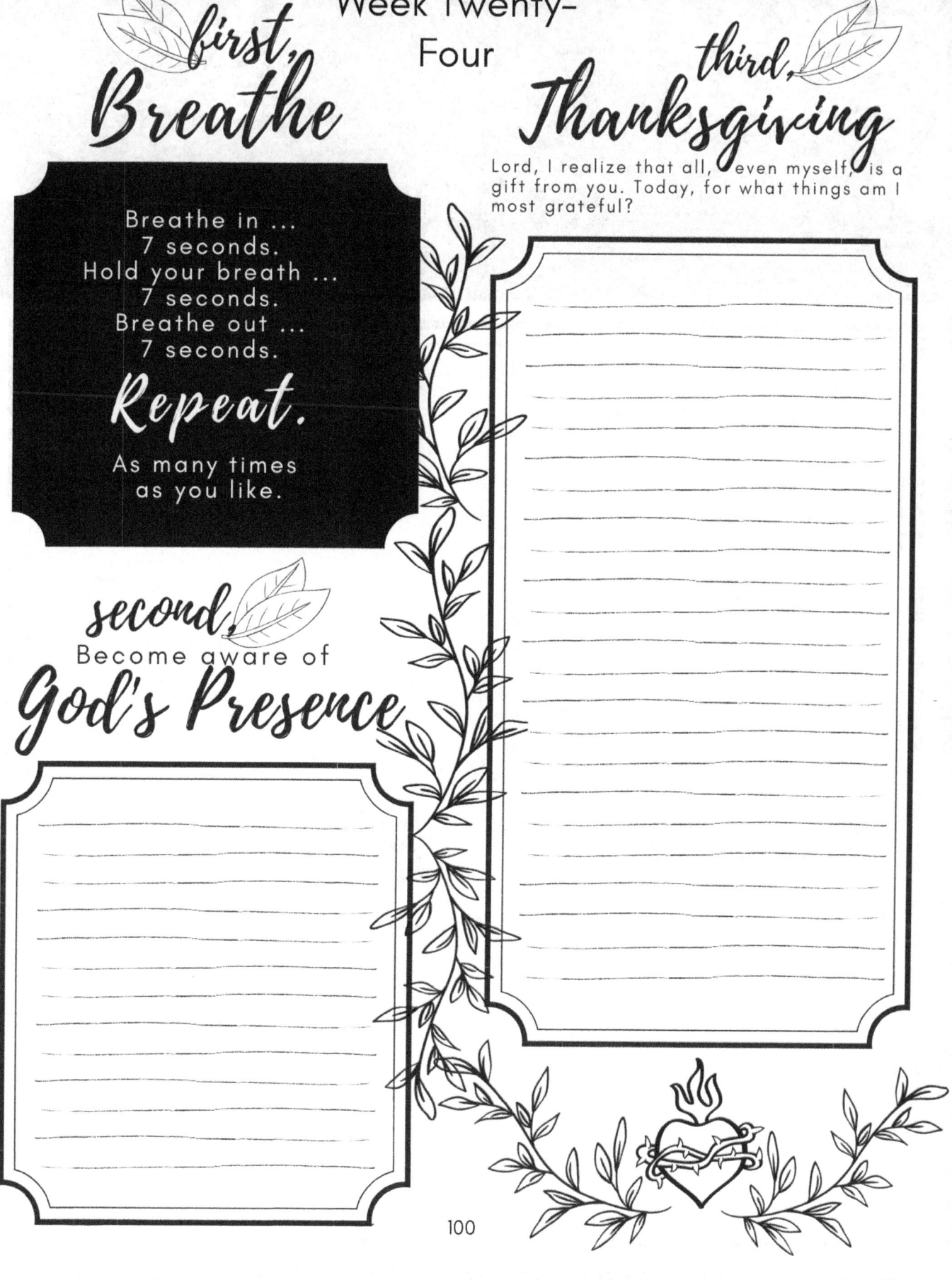

Week Twenty-Four

first, Breathe

Breathe in ... 7 seconds.
Hold your breath ... 7 seconds.
Breathe out ... 7 seconds.

Repeat. As many times as you like.

second, Become aware of God's Presence

third, Thanksgiving

Lord, I realize that all, even myself, is a gift from you. Today, for what things am I most grateful?

fourth, Reflect

*Do not let your hearts be troubled.
You believe in God; believe also in Me.*
John 14:1

fifth, Examination

Lord, open my eyes and ears to be more honest with myself. Show me what has been happening to me and in me this day. Today, how have I experienced your love?

sixth, Contrition

Today, what choices have been inadequate responses to your love?

seventh, Hope

Lord, let me look with longing toward the future. How will I let you lead me to a brighter tomorrow?

Weekly Prayer

A Celtic Prayer of Peace
David Adam

Calm me, Lord, as you calmed the storm;
Still me, Lord, keep me from harm.

Let all the tumult within me cease,
Enfold me, Lord, in your peace.

Calm me, Lord, as you calmed the storm;
Still me, Lord, keep me from harm.

Let all the tumult within me cease, Lord,
Enfold me in your peace.

Prayer Goals

Prayer Intentions

For whom or what do you want to pray this week? In particular, consider praying for those who frustrate or anger you, maybe even those who have harmed you or your loved ones.

_____
_____
_____
_____
_____
_____
_____
_____

As St. (Mother) Teresa said, "Not all of us can do great things. But we can do ... *small things with great love*"

List your "small things" below:

_____
_____
_____
_____
_____
_____
_____
_____
_____
_____
_____
_____

Goals Checklist

Don't feel like you need to check all these boxes every week. Start with a goal of perhaps 2 or 3 and build from there.

- [ ] Spiritual Reading
- [ ] Share your faith with someone
- [ ] Attend Church Services
- [ ] Pray with somebody
- [ ] Volunteer at Homeless Shelter or Food Bank
- [ ] Attend a Bible Study

Week Twenty-Five

first, Breathe

Breathe in ...
7 seconds.
Hold your breath ...
7 seconds.
Breathe out ...
7 seconds.

Repeat.

As many times as you like.

second, Become aware of God's Presence

third, Thanksgiving

Lord, I realize that all, even myself, is a gift from you. Today, for what things am I most grateful?

fourth, Reflect

> "Seen from the outside, all these trials are frightening. We wondered if we could ever confront anything similar. But each step is accompanied by a necessary grace."
> — Chiara Corbella Petrillo, *A Witness to Joy*

fifth, Examination

Lord, open my eyes and ears to be more honest with myself. Show me what has been happening to me and in me this day. Today, how have I experienced your love?

_____
_____
_____
_____
_____
_____
_____
_____

sixth, Contrition

Today, what choices have been inadequate responses to your love?

_____
_____
_____
_____
_____
_____
_____

seventh, Hope

Lord, let me look with longing toward the future. How will I let you lead me to a brighter tomorrow?

_____
_____
_____
_____
_____
_____
_____

Weekly Prayer

Prayer of Saint Richard of Chichester

Thanks be to thee,
My Lord Jesus Christ,
For all the benefits Thou hast given me,
For all the pains and insults
Thou hast borne for me.
O most merciful redeemer,
Friend and Brother,
May I know Thee more clearly,
Love Thee more dearly, and
Follow Thee more nearly,
Day by day.
Amen.

Prayer Goals

Prayer Intentions

For whom or what do you want to pray this week? In particular, consider praying for those who frustrate or anger you, maybe even those who have harmed you or your loved ones.

_____
_____
_____
_____
_____
_____
_____
_____

As St. (Mother) Teresa said, "Not all of us can do great things. But we can do ... *small things with great love*"

List your "small things" below:

Goals Checklist

Don't feel like you need to check all these boxes every week. Start with a goal of perhaps 2 or 3 and build from there.

- [ ] Spiritual Reading
- [ ] Share your faith with someone
- [ ] Attend Church Services
- [ ] Pray with somebody
- [ ] Volunteer at Homeless Shelter or Food Bank
- [ ] Attend a Bible Study

_____
_____
_____
_____
_____
_____
_____
_____
_____
_____
_____

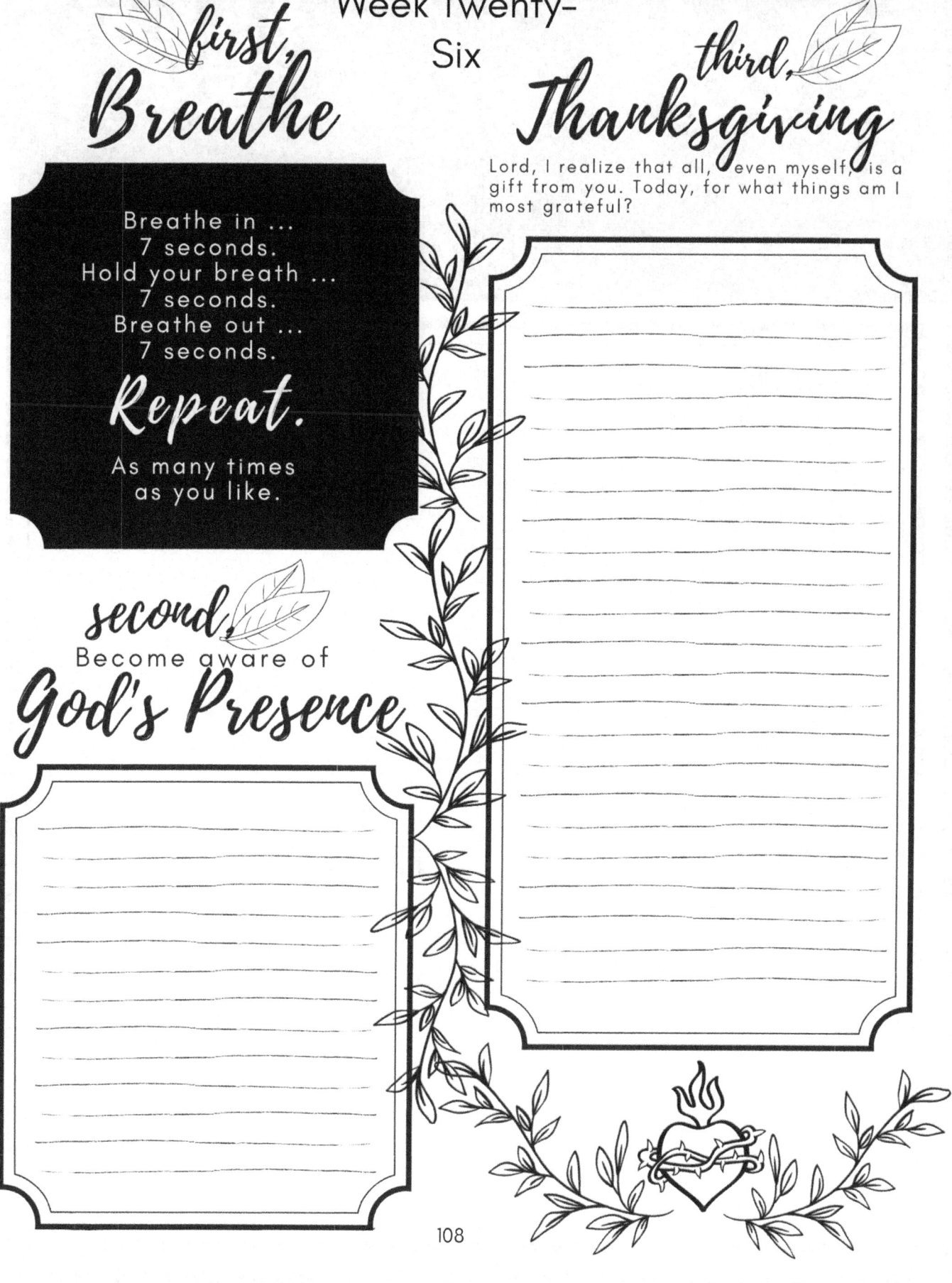

Week Twenty-Six

first, Breathe

Breathe in ... 7 seconds.
Hold your breath ... 7 seconds.
Breathe out ... 7 seconds.

Repeat. As many times as you like.

second, Become aware of God's Presence

third, Thanksgiving

Lord, I realize that all, even myself, is a gift from you. Today, for what things am I most grateful?

fourth, Reflect

For God has not given us a spirit of fear,
but of power and of love and of a sound mind.
2 Timothy 1:7

fifth, Examination

Lord, open my eyes and ears to be more honest with myself. Show me what has been happening to me and in me this day. Today, how have I experienced your love?

sixth, Contrition

Today, what choices have been inadequate responses to your love?

seventh, Hope

Lord, let me look with longing toward the future. How will I let you lead me to a brighter tomorrow?

Weekly Prayer

Holy Spirit Prayer of Saint Augustine

Breathe in me, O Holy Spirit,
That my thoughts may all be holy.
Act in me, O Holy Spirit,
That my work, too, may be holy.
Draw my heart, O Holy Spirit,
That I love but what is holy.
Strengthen me, O Holy Spirit,
To defend all that is holy.
Guard me, then, O Holy Spirit,
That I may always be holy.

Prayer Goals

Prayer Intentions

For whom or what do you want to pray this week? In particular, consider praying for those who frustrate or anger you, maybe even those who have harmed you or your loved ones.

As St. (Mother) Teresa said, "Not all of us can do great things. But we can do ... *small things with great love*"

List your "small things" below:

Goals Checklist

Don't feel like you need to check all these boxes every week. Start with a goal of perhaps 2 or 3 and build from there.

- [ ] Spiritual Reading
- [ ] Share your faith with someone
- [ ] Attend Church Services
- [ ] Pray with somebody
- [ ] Volunteer at Homeless Shelter or Food Bank
- [ ] Attend a Bible Study

Week Twenty-Seven

first, Breathe

Breathe in ...
7 seconds.
Hold your breath ...
7 seconds.
Breathe out ...
7 seconds.

Repeat.

As many times as you like.

second, Become aware of God's Presence

third, Thanksgiving

Lord, I realize that all, even myself, is a gift from you. Today, for what things am I most grateful?

fourth, Reflect

The Lord is my shepherd, I shall not want; He makes me lie down in green pastures. He leads me beside still waters; He restores my soul. He leads me in paths of righteousness for His name's sake.
Psalm 23:1-3

fifth, Examination

Lord, open my eyes and ears to be more honest with myself. Show me what has been happening to me and in me this day. Today, how have I experienced your love?

sixth, Contrition

Today, what choices have been inadequate responses to your love?

seventh, Hope

Lord, let me look with longing toward the future. How will I let you lead me to a brighter tomorrow?

Weekly Prayer

"Take and Receive" Prayer

Take, Lord, and receive all my liberty,
My memory, my understanding,
And my entire will –
All that I have and call my own.
You have given it all to me.
To you, Lord, I return it.
Everything is yours;
Do with it what you will.
Give me only your love and your grace.
That is enough for me.
Amen.

Prayer Goals

Prayer Intentions

For whom or what do you want to pray this week? In particular, consider praying for those who frustrate or anger you, maybe even those who have harmed you or your loved ones.

_____
_____
_____
_____
_____
_____
_____
_____

As St. (Mother) Teresa said, "Not all of us can do great things. But we can do ... *small things with great love*"

List your "small things" below:

_____
_____
_____
_____
_____
_____
_____
_____
_____
_____
_____

Goals Checklist

Don't feel like you need to check all these boxes every week. Start with a goal of perhaps 2 or 3 and build from there.

- [ ] Spiritual Reading
- [ ] Share your faith with someone
- [ ] Attend Church Services
- [ ] Pray with somebody
- [ ] Volunteer at Homeless Shelter or Food Bank
- [ ] Attend a Bible Study

Week Twenty-Eight

first, Breathe

Breathe in ... 7 seconds.
Hold your breath ... 7 seconds.
Breathe out ... 7 seconds.

Repeat.

As many times as you like.

second, Become aware of God's Presence

third, Thanksgiving

Lord, I realize that all, even myself, is a gift from you. Today, for what things am I most grateful?

fourth,
Reflect

Even though I walk through the valley of the shadow of death, I fear no evil; for Thou art with me; thy rod and thy staff, they comfort me.
Psalm 23:4

fifth, Examination

Lord, open my eyes and ears to be more honest with myself. Show me what has been happening to me and in me this day. Today, how have I experienced your love?

sixth, Contrition

Today, what choices have been inadequate responses to your love?

seventh, Hope

Lord, let me look with longing toward the future. How will I let you lead me to a brighter tomorrow?

Weekly Prayer

Act of Hope

My God, relying on your
infinite goodness and promises,
I hope to obtain pardon of my sins,
Help of your grace,
And life everlasting
Through the merits of Jesus Christ,
My Lord and Redeemer
Amen.

Prayer Goals

Prayer Intentions

For whom or what do you want to pray this week? In particular, consider praying for those who frustrate or anger you, maybe even those who have harmed you or your loved ones.

_____
_____
_____
_____
_____
_____
_____
_____

As St. (Mother) Teresa said, "Not all of us can do great things. But we can do ... *small things with great love*"

List your "small things" below:

_____
_____
_____
_____
_____
_____
_____
_____
_____
_____
_____

Goals Checklist

Don't feel like you need to check all these boxes every week. Start with a goal of perhaps 2 or 3 and build from there.

- [ ] Spiritual Reading
- [ ] Share your faith with someone
- [ ] Attend Church Services
- [ ] Pray with somebody
- [ ] Volunteer at Homeless Shelter or Food Bank
- [ ] Attend a Bible Study

Week Twenty-Nine

first, Breathe

Breathe in ...
7 seconds.
Hold your breath ...
7 seconds.
Breathe out ...
7 seconds.

Repeat.

As many times as you like.

second, Become aware of God's Presence

third, Thanksgiving

Lord, I realize that all, even myself, is a gift from you. Today, for what things am I most grateful?

fourth, Reflect

Then he placed his right hand on me and said:
"Do not be afraid. I am the First and the Last."
Revelation 1:17

fifth, Examination

Lord, open my eyes and ears to be more honest with myself. Show me what has been happening to me and in me this day. Today, how have I experienced your love?

sixth, Contrition

Today, what choices have been inadequate responses to your love?

seventh, Hope

Lord, let me look with longing toward the future. How will I let you lead me to a brighter tomorrow?

Weekly Prayer

Serenity Prayer

God, grant me the serenity
to accept the things I cannot change,
the courage to change the things I can,
and the wisdom to know the difference.
Living one day at a time,
enjoying one moment at a time;
accepting hardship as a pathway to peace;
taking, as Jesus did,
this sinful world as it is,
not as I would have it;
trusting that You will make all things right
if I surrender to Your will;
so that I may be reasonably happy in this life
and supremely happy with You
forever in the next.
Amen.

Prayer Goals

Prayer Intentions

For whom or what do you want to pray this week? In particular, consider praying for those who frustrate or anger you, maybe even those who have harmed you or your loved ones.

_____
_____
_____
_____
_____
_____
_____

As St. (Mother) Teresa said, "Not all of us can do great things. But we can do ... *small things with great love*"

List your "small things" below:

_____
_____
_____
_____
_____
_____
_____
_____
_____
_____

Goals Checklist

Don't feel like you need to check all these boxes every week. Start with a goal of perhaps 2 or 3 and build from there.

- ☐ Spiritual Reading
- ☐ Share your faith with someone
- ☐ Attend Church Services
- ☐ Pray with somebody
- ☐ Volunteer at Homeless Shelter or Food Bank
- ☐ Attend a Bible Study

Week Thirty

first, Breathe

Breathe in ...
7 seconds.
Hold your breath ...
7 seconds.
Breathe out ...
7 seconds.

Repeat.

As many times as you like.

second, Become aware of God's Presence

third, Thanksgiving

Lord, I realize that all, even myself, is a gift from you. Today, for what things am I most grateful?

fourth, Reflect

"Fear not, I am with you; be not dismayed; I am your God. I will strengthen you, and help you, and uphold you with my right hand of justice."
Isaiah 41:10

fifth, Examination

Lord, open my eyes and ears to be more honest with myself. Show me what has been happening to me and in me this day. Today, how have I experienced your love?

sixth, Contrition

Today, what choices have been inadequate responses to your love?

seventh, Hope

Lord, let me look with longing toward the future. How will I let you lead me to a brighter tomorrow?

Weekly Prayer

Litany of Humility

O Jesus, meek and humble of heart, *Hear me.*
From the desire of being esteemed, *Deliver me, O Jesus.*
From the desire of being loved, *Deliver me, O Jesus.*
From the desire of being extolled, *Deliver me, O Jesus.*
From the desire of being honored, *Deliver me, O Jesus.*
From the desire of being praised, *Deliver me, O Jesus.*
From the desire of being preferred to others, *Deliver me, O Jesus.*
From the desire of being consulted, *Deliver me, O Jesus.*
From the desire of being approved, *Deliver me, O Jesus.*
From the fear of being humiliated, *Deliver me, O Jesus.*
From the fear of being despised, *Deliver me, O Jesus.*
From the fear of suffering rebukes, *Deliver me, O Jesus.*
From the fear of being calumniated, *Deliver me, O Jesus.*
From the fear of being forgotten, *Deliver me, O Jesus.*
From the fear of being ridiculed, *Deliver me, O Jesus.*
From the fear of being wronged, *Deliver me, O Jesus.*
From the fear of being suspected, *Deliver me, O Jesus.*
That others may be loved more than I,
Jesus, grant me the grace to desire it.
That others may be esteemed more than I,
Jesus, grant me the grace to desire it.
That, in the opinion of the world, others may increase and I may decrease,
Jesus, grant me the grace to desire it.
That others may be chosen and I set aside,
Jesus, grant me the grace to desire it.
That others may be praised and I go unnoticed,
Jesus, grant me the grace to desire it.
That others may be preferred to me in everything,
Jesus, grant me the grace to desire it.
That others may become holier than I, provided that I may become as holy as I should, *Jesus, grant me the grace to desire it.*
Amen.

Prayer Goals

Prayer Intentions

For whom or what do you want to pray this week? In particular, consider praying for those who frustrate or anger you, maybe even those who have harmed you or your loved ones.

_____
_____
_____
_____
_____
_____
_____
_____

> As St. (Mother) Teresa said, "Not all of us can do great things. But we can do ... *small things with great love*"

List your "small things" below:

_____
_____
_____
_____
_____
_____
_____
_____
_____
_____

Goals Checklist

Don't feel like you need to check all these boxes every week. Start with a goal of perhaps 2 or 3 and build from there.

- [ ] Spiritual Reading
- [ ] Share your faith with someone
- [ ] Attend Church Services
- [ ] Pray with somebody
- [ ] Volunteer at Homeless Shelter or Food Bank
- [ ] Attend a Bible Study

Week Thirty-One

first, Breathe

Breathe in ...
7 seconds.
Hold your breath ...
7 seconds.
Breathe out ...
7 seconds.

Repeat.

As many times as you like.

second, Become aware of God's Presence

third, Thanksgiving

Lord, I realize that all, even myself, is a gift from you. Today, for what things am I most grateful?

fourth, Reflect

And I am convinced that nothing can ever separate us from God's love. Neither death nor life, neither angels nor demons, neither our fears for today nor our worries about tomorrow—not even the powers of hell can separate us from God's love.
Romans 8:38-39

fifth, Examination

Lord, open my eyes and ears to be more honest with myself. Show me what has been happening to me and in me this day. Today, how have I experienced your love?

sixth, Contrition

Today, what choices have been inadequate responses to your love?

seventh, Hope

Lord, let me look with longing toward the future. How will I let you lead me to a brighter tomorrow?

Weekly Prayer

Prayer for Calm

My Lord and my God,
I do not know what will happen to me today,
But what I do know is that
Nothing will happen to me today
That You and I together cannot handle.
This thought is enough
To bring me to face the day in peace.
I adore you in your wisdom and love.
I commend myself into your hands with the complete trust.
Amen.

Prayer Goals

Prayer Intentions

For whom or what do you want to pray this week? In particular, consider praying for those who frustrate or anger you, maybe even those who have harmed you or your loved ones.

_____
_____
_____
_____
_____
_____
_____
_____

> As St. (Mother) Teresa said, "Not all of us can do great things. But we can do ... *small things with great love*"

List your "small things" below:

_____
_____
_____
_____
_____
_____
_____
_____
_____
_____
_____
_____

Goals Checklist

Don't feel like you need to check all these boxes every week. Start with a goal of perhaps 2 or 3 and build from there.

- [ ] Spiritual Reading
- [ ] Share your faith with someone
- [ ] Attend Church Services
- [ ] Pray with somebody
- [ ] Volunteer at Homeless Shelter or Food Bank
- [ ] Attend a Bible Study

Week Thirty-Two

first, Breathe

Breathe in ... 7 seconds.
Hold your breath ... 7 seconds.
Breathe out ... 7 seconds.

Repeat. As many times as you like.

second, Become aware of God's Presence

third, Thanksgiving

Lord, I realize that all, even myself, is a gift from you. Today, for what things am I most grateful?

fourth, Reflect

"The Lord your God is in your midst, A victorious warrior. He will exult over you with joy, He will be quiet in His love, He will rejoice over you with shouts of joy."
Zephaniah 3:17

fifth, Examination

Lord, open my eyes and ears to be more honest with myself. Show me what has been happening to me and in me this day. Today, how have I experienced your love?

sixth, Contrition

Today, what choices have been inadequate responses to your love?

seventh, Hope

Lord, let me look with longing toward the future. How will I let you lead me to a brighter tomorrow?

Weekly Prayer

Litany of Trust, Part One
From the Sisters of Life

From the belief that I have to earn Your love,
Deliver me, Jesus.
From the fear that I am unlovable,
Deliver me, Jesus.
From the false security that I have what it takes,
Deliver me, Jesus.
From the fear that trusting You will leave me more destitute,
Deliver me, Jesus.
From all suspicion of Your words and promises,
Deliver me, Jesus.
From the rebellion against childlike dependency on You,
Deliver me, Jesus.
From refusals and reluctances in accepting Your will,
Deliver me, Jesus.
From anxiety about the future,
Deliver me, Jesus.
From resentment or excessive preoccupation with the past,
Deliver me, Jesus.
From restless self-seeking in the present moment,
Deliver me, Jesus.
From disbelief in Your love and presence,
Deliver me, Jesus.
From the fear of being asked to give more than I have,
Deliver me, Jesus.
From the belief that my life has no meaning or worth,
Deliver me, Jesus.
From the fear of what love demands,
Deliver me, Jesus.
From discouragement,
Deliver me. Jesus.

Prayer Goals

Prayer Intentions

For whom or what do you want to pray this week? In particular, consider praying for those who frustrate or anger you, maybe even those who have harmed you or your loved ones.

> As St. (Mother) Teresa said, "Not all of us can do great things. But we can do ... *small things with great love*"

List your "small things" below:

Goals Checklist

Don't feel like you need to check all these boxes every week. Start with a goal of perhaps 2 or 3 and build from there.

- [ ] Spiritual Reading
- [ ] Share your faith with someone
- [ ] Attend Church Services
- [ ] Pray with somebody
- [ ] Volunteer at Homeless Shelter or Food Bank
- [ ] Attend a Bible Study

Week Thirty-Three

first, Breathe

Breathe in …
7 seconds.
Hold your breath …
7 seconds.
Breathe out …
7 seconds.

Repeat.

As many times as you like.

second, Become aware of God's Presence

third, Thanksgiving

Lord, I realize that all, even myself, is a gift from you. Today, for what things am I most grateful?

fourth, Reflect

"Therefore I tell you, do not be anxious about your life, what you shall eat or what you shall drink, nor about your body, what you shall put on. Is not life more than food, and the body more than clothing? Look at the birds of the air: they neither sow nor reap nor gather into barns, and yet your heavenly Father feeds them. Are you not of more value than they? And which of you by being anxious can add one cubit to his span of life?"
Matthew 6:25-27

fifth, Examination

Lord, open my eyes and ears to be more honest with myself. Show me what has been happening to me and in me this day. Today, how have I experienced your love?

sixth, Contrition

Today, what choices have been inadequate responses to your love?

seventh, Hope

Lord, let me look with longing toward the future. How will I let you lead me to a brighter tomorrow?

Weekly Prayer

Litany of Trust, Part Two
From the Sisters of Life

That You are continually holding me, sustaining me, loving me,
Jesus, I trust in You.
That Your love goes deeper than my sins and failings and transforms me,
Jesus, I trust in You.
That not knowing what tomorrow brings is an invitation to lean on You,
Jesus, I trust in You.
That You are with me in my suffering, *Jesus, I trust in You.*
That my suffering, united to Your own, will bear fruit in this life and the next, *Jesus, I trust in You.*
That You will not leave me orphan, that You are present in Your Church,
Jesus, I trust in You.
That Your plan is better than anything else, *Jesus, I trust in You.*
That You always hear me and in Your goodness always respond to me
Jesus, I trust in You.
That You give me the grace to accept forgiveness and to forgive others
Jesus, I trust in You.
That You give me all the strength I need for what is asked
Jesus, I trust in You.
That my life is a gift, *Jesus, I trust in You.*
That You will teach me to trust You, *Jesus, I trust in You.*
That You are my Lord and my God, *Jesus, I trust in You.*
That I am Your beloved one, *Jesus, I trust in You.*

Prayer Goals

Prayer Intentions

For whom or what do you want to pray this week? In particular, consider praying for those who frustrate or anger you, maybe even those who have harmed you or your loved ones.

_____
_____
_____
_____
_____
_____
_____
_____
_____

As St. (Mother) Teresa said, "Not all of us can do great things. But we can do ... *small things with great love*"

List your "small things" below:

_____
_____
_____
_____
_____
_____
_____
_____
_____
_____
_____

Goals Checklist

Don't feel like you need to check all these boxes every week. Start with a goal of perhaps 2 or 3 and build from there.

- [ ] Spiritual Reading
- [ ] Share your faith with someone
- [ ] Attend Church Services
- [ ] Pray with somebody
- [ ] Volunteer at Homeless Shelter or Food Bank
- [ ] Attend a Bible Study

Week Thirty-Four

first, Breathe

Breathe in ...
7 seconds.
Hold your breath ...
7 seconds.
Breathe out ...
7 seconds.

Repeat.

As many times as you like.

second, Become aware of God's Presence

third, Thanksgiving

Lord, I realize that all, even myself, is a gift from you. Today, for what things am I most grateful?

fourth, Reflect

"And why are you anxious about clothing? Consider the lilies of the field, how they grow; they neither toil nor spin; yet I tell you, even Solomon in all his glory was not arrayed like one of these. But if God so clothes the grass of the field, which today is alive and tomorrow is thrown into the oven, will he not much more clothe you, O men of little faith?"
Matthew 6:28-30

fifth, Examination

Lord, open my eyes and ears to be more honest with myself. Show me what has been happening to me and in me this day. Today, how have I experienced your love?

_____
_____
_____
_____
_____
_____
_____
_____

sixth, Contrition

Today, what choices have been inadequate responses to your love?

_____
_____
_____
_____
_____
_____

seventh, Hope

Lord, let me look with longing toward the future. How will I let you lead me to a brighter tomorrow?

_____
_____
_____
_____
_____
_____

Weekly Prayer

Prayer for Peace and Calm
From John Greenleaf Whittier

Dear Lord and Father of humankind,
Forgive our foolish ways;
Reclothe us in our rightful mind,
In purer lives Thy service find,
In deeper reverence, praise.

Drop Thy still dews of quietness,
Till all our strivings cease;
Take from our souls the strain and stress,
And let our ordered lives confess
The beauty of Thy peace.

Breathe through the heats of our desire
Thy coolness and Thy balm;
Let sense be dumb, let flesh retire;
Speak through the earthquake, wind, and fire,
O still, small voice of calm.

Prayer Goals

Prayer Intentions

For whom or what do you want to pray this week? In particular, consider praying for those who frustrate or anger you, maybe even those who have harmed you or your loved ones.

_____
_____
_____
_____
_____
_____
_____

> As St. (Mother) Teresa said, "Not all of us can do great things. But we can do ... *small things with great love*"

List your "small things" below:

_____
_____
_____
_____
_____
_____
_____
_____
_____
_____

Goals Checklist

Don't feel like you need to check all these boxes every week. Start with a goal of perhaps 2 or 3 and build from there.

- ☐ Spiritual Reading
- ☐ Share your faith with someone
- ☐ Attend Church Services
- ☐ Pray with somebody
- ☐ Volunteer at Homeless Shelter or Food Bank
- ☐ Attend a Bible Study

Week Thirty-Five

first, Breathe

Breathe in ...
7 seconds.
Hold your breath ...
7 seconds.
Breathe out ...
7 seconds.

Repeat.

As many times as you like.

second, Become aware of God's Presence

third, Thanksgiving

Lord, I realize that all, even myself, is a gift from you. Today, for what things am I most grateful?

fourth, Reflect

*"Though an army encamp against me, my heart does not fear;
Though war be waged against me, even then do I trust."*
Psalm 27:3

fifth, Examination

Lord, open my eyes and ears to be more honest with myself. Show me what has been happening to me and in me this day. Today, how have I experienced your love?

sixth, Contrition

Today, what choices have been inadequate responses to your love?

seventh, Hope

Lord, let me look with longing toward the future. How will I let you lead me to a brighter tomorrow?

Weekly Prayer

A Prayer for Soothing Panic Attacks

Dear God,
I come before You to
Lay my panic and anxiety at Your feet.
When I'm crushed by my fears and worries,
remind me of Your power and Your grace.
Fill me with Your peace
As I trust in You and You alone.
I know I can't beat this on my own,
but I also know that I have You, Lord,
And You have already paid the ultimate price
To carry my burdens.
For this I thank you.
Amen.

Prayer Goals

Prayer Intentions

For whom or what do you want to pray this week? In particular, consider praying for those who frustrate or anger you, maybe even those who have harmed you or your loved ones.

_____
_____
_____
_____
_____
_____
_____
_____

> As St. (Mother) Teresa said, "Not all of us can do great things. But we can do ... *small things with great love*"

List your "small things" below:

_____
_____
_____
_____
_____
_____
_____
_____
_____
_____

Goals Checklist

Don't feel like you need to check all these boxes every week. Start with a goal of perhaps 2 or 3 and build from there.

- ☐ Spiritual Reading
- ☐ Share your faith with someone
- ☐ Attend Church Services
- ☐ Pray with somebody
- ☐ Volunteer at Homeless Shelter or Food Bank
- ☐ Attend a Bible Study

Week Thirty-Six

first, Breathe

Breathe in ...
7 seconds.
Hold your breath ...
7 seconds.
Breathe out ...
7 seconds.

Repeat.

As many times as you like.

second, Become aware of God's Presence

third, Thanksgiving

Lord, I realize that all, even myself, is a gift from you. Today, for what things am I most grateful?

fourth, Reflect

He who dwells in the shelter of the Most High will rest in the shadow of the Almighty. I will say of the Lord, "He is my refuge and my fortress, my God, in whom I trust."
Psalm 91:1-2

fifth, Examination

Lord, open my eyes and ears to be more honest with myself. Show me what has been happening to me and in me this day. Today, how have I experienced your love?

sixth, Contrition

Today, what choices have been inadequate responses to your love?

seventh, Hope

Lord, let me look with longing toward the future. How will I let you lead me to a brighter tomorrow?

Weekly Prayer

Your Peace

God,
Who is more than we can ever comprehend,
Help us to seek You,
And You alone.
Help us to stand before all that we could do
And seek what You would do,
And do that.
Lift from us our need
To achieve all that we can be
And instead,
Surrender to what You can be in us.
Give us ways to refrain from the busyness
That will put us on edge and off center,
Give us today Your peace.
Amen.

Prayer Goals

Prayer Intentions

For whom or what do you want to pray this week? In particular, consider praying for those who frustrate or anger you, maybe even those who have harmed you or your loved ones.

_____   _____
_____   _____
_____   _____
_____   _____
_____
_____
_____

> As St. (Mother) Teresa said, "Not all of us can do great things. But we can do … *small things with great love*"

List your "small things" below:

_____
_____
_____
_____

Goals Checklist

Don't feel like you need to check all these boxes every week. Start with a goal of perhaps 2 or 3 and build from there.

- ☐ Spiritual Reading
- ☐ Share your faith with someone
- ☐ Attend Church Services
- ☐ Pray with somebody
- ☐ Volunteer at Homeless Shelter or Food Bank
- ☐ Attend a Bible Study

Week Thirty-Seven

first, Breathe

Breathe in ... 7 seconds.
Hold your breath ... 7 seconds.
Breathe out ... 7 seconds.

Repeat.

As many times as you like.

second, Become aware of God's Presence

third, Thanksgiving

Lord, I realize that all, even myself, is a gift from you. Today, for what things am I most grateful?

fourth, Reflect

> He will cover you with His feathers, and under His wings you will find refuge; His faithfulness will be your shield and rampart. You will not fear the terror of night, nor the arrow that flies by day, nor the pestilence that stalks in the darkness, nor the plague that destroys at midday. A thousand may fall at your side, ten thousand at your right hand, but it will not come near you.
> Psalm 91:4-7

fifth, Examination

Lord, open my eyes and ears to be more honest with myself. Show me what has been happening to me and in me this day. Today, how have I experienced your love?

sixth, Contrition

Today, what choices have been inadequate responses to your love?

seventh, Hope

Lord, let me look with longing toward the future. How will I let you lead me to a brighter tomorrow?

Weekly *Prayer*

Prayer for Strength
From Psalm 27:1b

Dear Jesus,
You are the strength of my life;
You are my rock, my fortress and my protector;
Therefore, whom shall I be afraid?
You are my shield,
My strong-tower and my stronghold.
I will call to You because
You are worthy to be praised.
So, Father,
I thank you for being my strength
And My God in whom I trust.
Amen.

Prayer Goals

Prayer Intentions

For whom or what do you want to pray this week? In particular, consider praying for those who frustrate or anger you, maybe even those who have harmed you or your loved ones.

_____
_____
_____
_____
_____
_____
_____
_____

> As St. (Mother) Teresa said, "Not all of us can do great things. But we can do … *small things with great love*"

List your "small things" below:

_____
_____
_____
_____
_____
_____
_____
_____
_____
_____
_____
_____

Goals Checklist

Don't feel like you need to check all these boxes every week. Start with a goal of perhaps 2 or 3 and build from there.

- ☐ Spiritual Reading
- ☐ Share your faith with someone
- ☐ Attend Church Services
- ☐ Pray with somebody
- ☐ Volunteer at Homeless Shelter or Food Bank
- ☐ Attend a Bible Study

Week Thirty-Eight

first, Breathe

Breathe in ...
7 seconds.
Hold your breath ...
7 seconds.
Breathe out ...
7 seconds.

Repeat.

As many times as you like.

second, Become aware of God's Presence

third, Thanksgiving

Lord, I realize that all, even myself, is a gift from you. Today, for what things am I most grateful?

fourth, Reflect

For He will command His angels concerning you, to guard you in all your ways. On their hands they will bear you up, lest you dash your foot against a stone.
Psalm 91:11-12

fifth, Examination

Lord, open my eyes and ears to be more honest with myself. Show me what has been happening to me and in me this day. Today, how have I experienced your love?

sixth, Contrition

Today, what choices have been inadequate responses to your love?

seventh, Hope

Lord, let me look with longing toward the future. How will I let you lead me to a brighter tomorrow?

Weekly Prayer

Prayer of St. Francis

Lord, make me an instrument of your peace:
where there is hatred, let me sow love;
where there is injury, pardon;
where there is doubt, faith;
where there is despair, hope;
where there is darkness, light;
where there is sadness, joy.

O divine Master, grant that I may not so much seek
to be consoled as to console,
to be understood as to understand,
to be loved as to love.
For it is in giving that we receive,
it is in pardoning that we are pardoned,
and it is in dying that we are born to eternal life.
Amen.

Prayer Goals

Prayer Intentions

For whom or what do you want to pray this week? In particular, consider praying for those who frustrate or anger you, maybe even those who have harmed you or your loved ones.

_____
_____
_____
_____
_____
_____
_____
_____

> As St. (Mother) Teresa said, "Not all of us can do great things. But we can do ... *small things with great love*"

List your "small things" below:

_____
_____
_____
_____
_____
_____
_____
_____
_____

Goals Checklist

Don't feel like you need to check all these boxes every week. Start with a goal of perhaps 2 or 3 and build from there.

- [ ] Spiritual Reading
- [ ] Share your faith with someone
- [ ] Attend Church Services
- [ ] Pray with somebody
- [ ] Volunteer at Homeless Shelter or Food Bank
- [ ] Attend a Bible Study

Week Thirty-Nine

first, Breathe

Breathe in ... 7 seconds.
Hold your breath ... 7 seconds.
Breathe out ... 7 seconds.

Repeat.

As many times as you like.

second, Become aware of God's Presence

third, Thanksgiving

Lord, I realize that all, even myself, is a gift from you. Today, for what things am I most grateful?

fourth, Reflect

"Because he loves me," says the Lord, "I will rescue him; I will protect him, for he acknowledges My Name. He will call upon Me, and I will answer him; I will be with him in trouble, I will deliver him and honor him."
Psalm 91:14-15

fifth, Examination

Lord, open my eyes and ears to be more honest with myself. Show me what has been happening to me and in me this day. Today, how have I experienced your love?

sixth, Contrition

Today, what choices have been inadequate responses to your love?

seventh, Hope

Lord, let me look with longing toward the future. How will I let you lead me to a brighter tomorrow?

Weekly Prayer

I Want To Be Available

Holy and perfect God,
You know I want to be available.
Help that desire sink deeply enough
Into my being
For me to actually change
And to say "no" to a least one worthy,
But not urgent, task today.
Give me the ability to be open
To the life I am leading;
Not the one I am planning to lead.

Prayer Goals

Prayer Intentions

For whom or what do you want to pray this week? In particular, consider praying for those who frustrate or anger you, maybe even those who have harmed you or your loved ones.

_____
_____
_____
_____
_____
_____
_____
_____
_____

> As St. (Mother) Teresa said, "Not all of us can do great things. But we can do ... *small things with great love*"

List your "small things" below:

_____
_____
_____
_____
_____
_____
_____
_____
_____
_____
_____

Goals Checklist

Don't feel like you need to check all these boxes every week. Start with a goal of perhaps 2 or 3 and build from there.

- ☐ Spiritual Reading
- ☐ Share your faith with someone
- ☐ Attend Church Services
- ☐ Pray with somebody
- ☐ Volunteer at Homeless Shelter or Food Bank
- ☐ Attend a Bible Study

Week Forty

first, Breathe

Breathe in ... 7 seconds.
Hold your breath ... 7 seconds.
Breathe out ... 7 seconds.

Repeat.

As many times as you like.

second, Become aware of God's Presence

third, Thanksgiving

Lord, I realize that all, even myself, is a gift from you. Today, for what things am I most grateful?

fourth, Reflect

Bear with each other and forgive one another if any of you has a grievance against someone. Forgive as the Lord forgave you.
Colossians 3:13

fifth, Examination

Lord, open my eyes and ears to be more honest with myself. Show me what has been happening to me and in me this day. Today, how have I experienced your love?

sixth, Contrition

Today, what choices have been inadequate responses to your love?

seventh, Hope

Lord, let me look with longing toward the future. How will I let you lead me to a brighter tomorrow?

Weekly Prayer

A Prayer for Calming a Troubled Heart

Loving God,
Please grant me peace of mind
And calm my troubled heart.
My soul is like a turbulent sea.
I can't seem to find my balance,
So I stumble and worry constantly.

Give me the strength and clarity of mind
To find my purpose and walk the path
You've laid out for me.
I trust Your Love, God,
And know that You will heal this stress.
Just as the sun rises each day
Against the dark of night.
Please bring me clarity with the light of God.
In Your Name I pray.
Amen.

Prayer Goals

Prayer Intentions

For whom or what do you want to pray this week? In particular, consider praying for those who frustrate or anger you, maybe even those who have harmed you or your loved ones.

As St. (Mother) Teresa said, "Not all of us can do great things. But we can do ... *small things with great love*"

List your "small things" below:

Goals Checklist

Don't feel like you need to check all these boxes every week. Start with a goal of perhaps 2 or 3 and build from there.

- [ ] Spiritual Reading
- [ ] Share your faith with someone
- [ ] Attend Church Services
- [ ] Pray with somebody
- [ ] Volunteer at Homeless Shelter or Food Bank
- [ ] Attend a Bible Study

Week Forty-One

first, Breathe

Breathe in ...
7 seconds.
Hold your breath ...
7 seconds.
Breathe out ...
7 seconds.

Repeat.

As many times as you like.

second, Become aware of God's Presence

third, Thanksgiving

Lord, I realize that all, even myself, is a gift from you. Today, for what things am I most grateful?

fourth, Reflect

Peace I leave with you; my peace I give to you; not as the world gives do I give to you. Let not your hearts be troubled, neither let them be afraid.
John 14:27

fifth, Examination

Lord, open my eyes and ears to be more honest with myself. Show me what has been happening to me and in me this day. Today, how have I experienced your love?

sixth, Contrition

Today, what choices have been inadequate responses to your love?

seventh, Hope

Lord, let me look with longing toward the future. How will I let you lead me to a brighter tomorrow?

Weekly Prayer

A Prayer for Christ's Peace

Lord, please put Your peace in my heart.
I'm worried and anxious.
My mind races and obsesses.
I can't help thinking about my problems.
And the more I think about them,
The more depressed I become.
I feel like I'm sinking down in quicksand
And can't get out.
Calm me, Lord.
Slow me down,
Put Your peace in my heart.

No matter what problem I have, Lord,
You are bigger,
You are more powerful than it is.
So I bring my problem to You.
I know what I want.
I know my will, but I do not know Yours.
I do not know how You will use this problem for my salvation.
I do not know what good You will work from this evil.
But I trust You.
I trust Your goodness and Your wisdom.
So I place myself in Your hands.
Please fill my heart with peace.
Amen.

Prayer Goals

Prayer Intentions

For whom or what do you want to pray this week? In particular, consider praying for those who frustrate or anger you, maybe even those who have harmed you or your loved ones.

_____
_____
_____
_____
_____
_____
_____
_____

> As St. (Mother) Teresa said, "Not all of us can do great things. But we can do ... *small things with great love*"

List your "small things" below:

_____
_____
_____
_____
_____
_____
_____
_____
_____
_____

Goals Checklist

Don't feel like you need to check all these boxes every week. Start with a goal of perhaps 2 or 3 and build from there.

- ☐ Spiritual Reading
- ☐ Share your faith with someone
- ☐ Attend Church Services
- ☐ Pray with somebody
- ☐ Volunteer at Homeless Shelter or Food Bank
- ☐ Attend a Bible Study

Week Forty-Two

first, Breathe

Breathe in ... 7 seconds.
Hold your breath ... 7 seconds.
Breathe out ... 7 seconds.

Repeat.

As many times as you like.

second, Become aware of God's Presence

third, Thanksgiving

Lord, I realize that all, even myself, is a gift from you. Today, for what things am I most grateful?

fourth, Reflect

Get rid of all bitterness, rage, and anger, brawling and slander, along with every form of malice. Be kind and compassionate to one another, forgiving each other, just as in Christ God forgave you.
Ephesians 4:31-32

fifth, Examination

Lord, open my eyes and ears to be more honest with myself. Show me what has been happening to me and in me this day. Today, how have I experienced your love?

sixth, Contrition

Today, what choices have been inadequate responses to your love?

seventh, Hope

Lord, let me look with longing toward the future. How will I let you lead me to a brighter tomorrow?

Weekly Prayer

Anima Christi

Soul of Christ, *sanctify me.*
Body of Christ, *save me.*
Blood of Christ, *inebriate me.*
Water from the side of Christ, *wash me.*
Passion of Christ, *strengthen me.*
O Good Jesus, *hear me.*
Within your wounds, *hide me.*
Permit me not to be separated from you.
From the wicked foe, *defend me.*
At the hour of my death, *call me*
And bid me come to you,
That with your saints I may praise you
Forever and ever.
Amen.

Prayer Goals

Prayer Intentions

For whom or what do you want to pray this week? In particular, consider praying for those who frustrate or anger you, maybe even those who have harmed you or your loved ones.

_____
_____
_____
_____
_____
_____
_____

> As St. (Mother) Teresa said, "Not all of us can do great things. But we can do ... *small things with great love*"

List your "small things" below:

_____
_____
_____
_____
_____
_____
_____
_____
_____
_____

Goals Checklist

Don't feel like you need to check all these boxes every week. Start with a goal of perhaps 2 or 3 and build from there.

- [ ] Spiritual Reading
- [ ] Share your faith with someone
- [ ] Attend Church Services
- [ ] Pray with somebody
- [ ] Volunteer at Homeless Shelter or Food Bank
- [ ] Attend a Bible Study

Week Forty-Three

first, Breathe

Breathe in … 7 seconds.
Hold your breath … 7 seconds.
Breathe out … 7 seconds.

Repeat.

As many times as you like.

second, Become aware of God's Presence

third, Thanksgiving

Lord, I realize that all, even myself, is a gift from you. Today, for what things am I most grateful?

fourth, Reflect

For I know the plans I have for you, says the Lord, plans for welfare and not for evil, to give you a future and a hope.
Jeremiah 29:11

fifth, Examination

Lord, open my eyes and ears to be more honest with myself. Show me what has been happening to me and in me this day. Today, how have I experienced your love?

sixth, Contrition

Today, what choices have been inadequate responses to your love?

seventh, Hope

Lord, let me look with longing toward the future. How will I let you lead me to a brighter tomorrow?

Weekly Prayer

A Prayer for Hope

Dear Lord,
I am your humble servant and
I kneel before You today,
Helpless and weak.
I need Your hope for love,
Kindness and for a better life, Lord.
I ask that You fill me from head to toe
With Your everlasting light.
Bathe me in Your glory, Lord,
And show me that everything is
According to Your plan.
Help me walk in Your glorious light and
Show me the path,
So that I may follow You in faith.
Amen.

Prayer Goals

Prayer Intentions

For whom or what do you want to pray this week? In particular, consider praying for those who frustrate or anger you, maybe even those who have harmed you or your loved ones.

_____
_____
_____
_____
_____
_____
_____
_____

> As St. (Mother) Teresa said, "Not all of us can do great things. But we can do … *small things with great love*"

List your "small things" below:

_____
_____
_____
_____
_____
_____
_____
_____
_____
_____

Goals Checklist

Don't feel like you need to check all these boxes every week. Start with a goal of perhaps 2 or 3 and build from there.

- ☐ Spiritual Reading
- ☐ Share your faith with someone
- ☐ Attend Church Services
- ☐ Pray with somebody
- ☐ Volunteer at Homeless Shelter or Food Bank
- ☐ Attend a Bible Study

Week Forty-Four

first, Breathe

Breathe in … 7 seconds.
Hold your breath … 7 seconds.
Breathe out … 7 seconds.

Repeat. As many times as you like.

second, Become aware of God's Presence

third, Thanksgiving

Lord, I realize that all, even myself, is a gift from you. Today, for what things am I most grateful?

fourth, Reflect

If we confess our sins, He is faithful and just
and will forgive us our sins and purify us from all unrighteousness.
1 John 1:19

fifth, Examination

Lord, open my eyes and ears to be more honest with myself. Show me what has been happening to me and in me this day. Today, how have I experienced your love?

sixth, Contrition

Today, what choices have been inadequate responses to your love?

seventh, Hope

Lord, let me look with longing toward the future. How will I let you lead me to a brighter tomorrow?

Weekly Prayer

A Prayer to Cast Out Fear

I know that worrying gets me nowhere.
Yet I still allow worry and anxiety to consume me.
In times such as these,
Lord Jesus,
I ask you to grant me
A great amount of strength, faith, and courage
To fight off the doubt and fear
Within my mind and heart.
Faith casts out fear
While fear casts out faith.

Prayer Goals

Prayer Intentions

For whom or what do you want to pray this week? In particular, consider praying for those who frustrate or anger you, maybe even those who have harmed you or your loved ones.

_____
_____
_____
_____
_____
_____
_____

As St. (Mother) Teresa said, "Not all of us can do great things. But we can do ... *small things with great love*"

List your "small things" below:

_____
_____
_____
_____

Goals Checklist

Don't feel like you need to check all these boxes every week. Start with a goal of perhaps 2 or 3 and build from there.

- ☐ Spiritual Reading
- ☐ Share your faith with someone
- ☐ Attend Church Services
- ☐ Pray with somebody
- ☐ Volunteer at Homeless Shelter or Food Bank
- ☐ Attend a Bible Study

_____
_____
_____
_____
_____
_____

Week Forty-Five

first, Breathe

Breathe in … 7 seconds.
Hold your breath … 7 seconds.
Breathe out … 7 seconds.

Repeat.

As many times as you like.

second, Become aware of God's Presence

third, Thanksgiving

Lord, I realize that all, even myself, is a gift from you. Today, for what things am I most grateful?

fourth, Reflect

He will deliver my soul in safety from the battle that I wage, for many are arrayed against me.
Psalm 55:18

fifth, Examination

Lord, open my eyes and ears to be more honest with myself. Show me what has been happening to me and in me this day. Today, how have I experienced your love?

_____
_____
_____
_____
_____
_____
_____
_____
_____

sixth, Contrition

Today, what choices have been inadequate responses to your love?

_____
_____
_____
_____
_____
_____
_____

seventh, Hope

Lord, let me look with longing toward the future. How will I let you lead me to a brighter tomorrow?

_____
_____
_____
_____
_____
_____
_____

Weekly Prayer

A Prayer for the Weary

Father, my heart is heavy.
I feel like I have to carry the burden alone.
Words like overwhelmed, distraught, exhausted
Seem to describe where I am.
I am not sure how to let you carry my heavy
Load, so please show me how.
Take it from me.
Let me rest and be refreshed
So that my heart won't be
So heavy in the morning.
In Jesus' name.
Amen.

Prayer Goals

Prayer Intentions

For whom or what do you want to pray this week? In particular, consider praying for those who frustrate or anger you, maybe even those who have harmed you or your loved ones.

> As St. (Mother) Teresa said, "Not all of us can do great things. But we can do ... *small things with great love*"

List your "small things" below:

Goals Checklist

Don't feel like you need to check all these boxes every week. Start with a goal of perhaps 2 or 3 and build from there.

- ☐ Spiritual Reading
- ☐ Share your faith with someone
- ☐ Attend Church Services
- ☐ Pray with somebody
- ☐ Volunteer at Homeless Shelter or Food Bank
- ☐ Attend a Bible Study

Week Forty-Six

first, Breathe

Breathe in ... 7 seconds.
Hold your breath ... 7 seconds.
Breathe out ... 7 seconds.

Repeat.

As many times as you like.

second, Become aware of God's Presence

third, Thanksgiving

Lord, I realize that all, even myself, is a gift from you. Today, for what things am I most grateful?

fourth, Reflect

Repent, then, and turn to God, so that your sins may be wiped out, that times of refreshing may come from the Lord.
Acts 3:19

fifth, Examination

Lord, open my eyes and ears to be more honest with myself. Show me what has been happening to me and in me this day. Today, how have I experienced your love?

_____
_____
_____
_____
_____
_____
_____
_____

sixth, Contrition

Today, what choices have been inadequate responses to your love?

_____
_____
_____
_____
_____
_____

seventh, Hope

Lord, let me look with longing toward the future. How will I let you lead me to a brighter tomorrow?

_____
_____
_____
_____
_____
_____

Weekly Prayer

A Prayer for
Letting Go of Worries

Heavenly Father,
Lately I've been so worried about
Things that are out of my control.
Help me to trust that
You are working out
Every little detail of my life and
That I have nothing to fear
Or worry about.
In Jesus' name,
Amen.

Prayer Goals

Prayer Intentions

For whom or what do you want to pray this week? In particular, consider praying for those who frustrate or anger you, maybe even those who have harmed you or your loved ones.

_____
_____
_____
_____
_____
_____
_____
_____

As St. (Mother) Teresa said, "Not all of us can do great things. But we can do ... *small things with great love*"

List your "small things" below:

_____
_____
_____
_____
_____
_____
_____
_____
_____
_____

Goals Checklist

Don't feel like you need to check all these boxes every week. Start with a goal of perhaps 2 or 3 and build from there.

- [ ] Spiritual Reading
- [ ] Share your faith with someone
- [ ] Attend Church Services
- [ ] Pray with somebody
- [ ] Volunteer at Homeless Shelter or Food Bank
- [ ] Attend a Bible Study

Week Forty-Seven

first, Breathe

Breathe in ... 7 seconds.
Hold your breath ... 7 seconds.
Breathe out ... 7 seconds.

Repeat.

As many times as you like.

second, Become aware of God's Presence

third, Thanksgiving

Lord, I realize that all, even myself, is a gift from you. Today, for what things am I most grateful?

fourth, Reflect

"Come now, let us settle the matter," says the LORD.
"Though your sins are like scarlet, they shall be as white as snow;
though they are red as crimson, they shall be like wool."
Isaiah 1:18

fifth, Examination

Lord, open my eyes and ears to be more honest with myself. Show me what has been happening to me and in me this day. Today, how have I experienced your love?

sixth, Contrition

Today, what choices have been inadequate responses to your love?

seventh, Hope

Lord, let me look with longing toward the future. How will I let you lead me to a brighter tomorrow?

Weekly Prayer

Magnificat

My soul proclaims the greatness of the Lord,
My spirit rejoices in God my Savior;
For he has looked with favor on his lowly servant.
From this day all generations will call me blessed:
The Almighty has done great things for me,
And holy is his Name.
He has mercy on those who fear him
in every generation.
He has shown the strength of his arm,
He has scattered the proud in their conceit.
He has cast down the mighty from their thrones,
And has lifted up the lowly.
He has filled the hungry with good things,
And the rich he has sent away empty.
He has come to the help of his servant Israel
For he has remembered his promise of mercy,
The promise he made to our fathers,
To Abraham and his children forever.

Prayer Goals

Prayer Intentions

For whom or what do you want to pray this week? In particular, consider praying for those who frustrate or anger you, maybe even those who have harmed you or your loved ones.

_____
_____
_____
_____
_____
_____
_____

As St. (Mother) Teresa said, "Not all of us can do great things. But we can do ... *small things with great love*"

List your "small things" below:

_____
_____
_____
_____
_____
_____
_____
_____
_____
_____
_____

Goals Checklist

Don't feel like you need to check all these boxes every week. Start with a goal of perhaps 2 or 3 and build from there.

- [ ] Spiritual Reading
- [ ] Share your faith with someone
- [ ] Attend Church Services
- [ ] Pray with somebody
- [ ] Volunteer at Homeless Shelter or Food Bank
- [ ] Attend a Bible Study

Week Forty-Eight

first, Breathe

Breathe in ...
7 seconds.
Hold your breath ...
7 seconds.
Breathe out ...
7 seconds.

Repeat.

As many times as you like.

second, Become aware of God's Presence

third, Thanksgiving

Lord, I realize that all, even myself, is a gift from you. Today, for what things am I most grateful?

fourth, Reflect

"Come to me, all who labor and are heavy laden, and I will give you rest. Take my yoke upon you, and learn from me; for I am gentle and lowly in heart, and you will find rest for your souls. For my yoke is easy, and my burden is light."
Matthew 11:28-30

fifth, Examination

Lord, open my eyes and ears to be more honest with myself. Show me what has been happening to me and in me this day. Today, how have I experienced your love?

sixth, Contrition

Today, what choices have been inadequate responses to your love?

seventh, Hope

Lord, let me look with longing toward the future. How will I let you lead me to a brighter tomorrow?

Weekly Prayer

A Prayer for Unburdening the Mind

Dear Loving Lord,
I am feeling stress, I am worried.
Too many things occupy my mind.
Won't you help me?
Show me, Lord,
Your order and Your plans are eternal.
Let me trust in Your Will alone.
Your Word tells me where there is love,
there is no fear.
Let me be filled with Your Love.
The perfect love
That tells me I am not condemned,
but I am saved.
I can do all things through You.
You strengthen me.
In Jesus name,
Amen.

Prayer Goals

Prayer Intentions

For whom or what do you want to pray this week? In particular, consider praying for those who frustrate or anger you, maybe even those who have harmed you or your loved ones.

_____
_____
_____
_____
_____
_____
_____
_____

As St. (Mother) Teresa said, "Not all of us can do great things. But we can do ... *small things with great love*"

List your "small things" below:

_____
_____
_____
_____
_____
_____
_____
_____
_____
_____

Goals Checklist

Don't feel like you need to check all these boxes every week. Start with a goal of perhaps 2 or 3 and build from there.

- ☐ Spiritual Reading
- ☐ Share your faith with someone
- ☐ Attend Church Services
- ☐ Pray with somebody
- ☐ Volunteer at Homeless Shelter or Food Bank
- ☐ Attend a Bible Study

Week Forty-Nine

first, Breathe

Breathe in ... 7 seconds.
Hold your breath ... 7 seconds.
Breathe out ... 7 seconds.

Repeat.

As many times as you like.

second, Become aware of God's Presence

third, Thanksgiving

Lord, I realize that all, even myself, is a gift from you. Today, for what things am I most grateful?

Strengthen the weak hands, and make firm the feeble knees. Say to those who are of a fearful heart, "Be strong, fear not! Behold, your God will come with vengeance, with the recompense of God. He will come and save you.
Isaiah 35:4

fifth, Examination

Lord, open my eyes and ears to be more honest with myself. Show me what has been happening to me and in me this day. Today, how have I experienced your love?

_____
_____
_____
_____
_____
_____
_____
_____

sixth, Contrition

Today, what choices have been inadequate responses to your love?

_____
_____
_____
_____
_____

seventh, Hope

Lord, let me look with longing toward the future. How will I let you lead me to a brighter tomorrow?

_____
_____
_____
_____
_____

Weekly Prayer

St. Francis' Canticle of the Sun

Be praised, my Lord,
For all your creatures,
And first for brother sun,
Who makes the day bright and luminous.
He is beautiful and radiant
With great splendor
He is the image of You,
Most high.
Be praised, my Lord,
For sister moon and the stars.
You placed them in the sky,
So bright and twinkling.

Prayer Goals

Prayer Intentions

For whom or what do you want to pray this week? In particular, consider praying for those who frustrate or anger you, maybe even those who have harmed you or your loved ones.

_____
_____
_____
_____
_____
_____
_____
_____

As St. (Mother) Teresa said, "Not all of us can do great things. But we can do ... *small things with great love*"

List your "small things" below:

_____
_____
_____
_____
_____
_____
_____
_____
_____
_____

Goals Checklist

Don't feel like you need to check all these boxes every week. Start with a goal of perhaps 2 or 3 and build from there.

- ☐ Spiritual Reading
- ☐ Share your faith with someone
- ☐ Attend Church Services
- ☐ Pray with somebody
- ☐ Volunteer at Homeless Shelter or Food Bank
- ☐ Attend a Bible Study

Week Fifty

first, Breathe

Breathe in ... 7 seconds.
Hold your breath ... 7 seconds.
Breathe out ... 7 seconds.

Repeat.

As many times as you like.

second, Become aware of God's Presence

third, Thanksgiving

Lord, I realize that all, even myself, is a gift from you. Today, for what things am I most grateful?

fourth, Reflect

In Him, we have redemption through His blood, the forgiveness of sins, in accordance with the riches of God's grace.
Ephesians 1:7

fifth, Examination

Lord, open my eyes and ears to be more honest with myself. Show me what has been happening to me and in me this day. Today, how have I experienced your love?

sixth, Contrition

Today, what choices have been inadequate responses to your love?

seventh, Hope

Lord, let me look with longing toward the future. How will I let you lead me to a brighter tomorrow?

Weekly Prayer

A Celtic Prayer of Peace
David Adam

Calm me, Lord, as you calmed the storm;
Still me, Lord, keep me from harm.

Let all the tumult within me cease,
Enfold me, Lord, in your peace.

Calm me, Lord, as you calmed the storm;
Still me, Lord, keep me from harm.

Let all the tumult within me cease, Lord,
Enfold me in your peace.

Prayer Goals

Prayer Intentions

For whom or what do you want to pray this week? In particular, consider praying for those who frustrate or anger you, maybe even those who have harmed you or your loved ones.

_____
_____
_____
_____
_____
_____
_____
_____

> As St. (Mother) Teresa said, "Not all of us can do great things. But we can do ... *small things with great love*"

List your "small things" below:

_____
_____
_____
_____
_____
_____
_____
_____
_____

Goals Checklist

Don't feel like you need to check all these boxes every week. Start with a goal of perhaps 2 or 3 and build from there.

- [ ] Spiritual Reading
- [ ] Share your faith with someone
- [ ] Attend Church Services
- [ ] Pray with somebody
- [ ] Volunteer at Homeless Shelter or Food Bank
- [ ] Attend a Bible Study

Week Fifty-One

first, Breathe

Breathe in ... 7 seconds.
Hold your breath ... 7 seconds.
Breathe out ... 7 seconds.

Repeat.

As many times as you like.

second, Become aware of God's Presence

third, Thanksgiving

Lord, I realize that all, even myself, is a gift from you. Today, for what things am I most grateful?

fourth, Reflect

Truly, truly, I say to you, he who believes has eternal life. I am the bread of life. Your fathers ate the manna in the wilderness, and they died. This is the bread which comes down from heaven, that a man may eat of it and not die. I am the living bread which came down from heaven; if anyone eats of this bread, he will live forever; and the bread which I shall give for the life of the world is my flesh.
John 6:47-51

fifth, Examination

Lord, open my eyes and ears to be more honest with myself. Show me what has been happening to me and in me this day. Today, how have I experienced your love?

sixth, Contrition

Today, what choices have been inadequate responses to your love?

seventh, Hope

Lord, let me look with longing toward the future. How will I let you lead me to a brighter tomorrow?

Weekly Prayer

Prayer of Saint Richard of Chichester

Thanks be to thee,
My Lord Jesus Christ,
For all the benefits Thou hast given me,
For all the pains and insults
Thou hast borne for me.
O most merciful redeemer,
Friend and Brother,
May I know Thee more clearly,
Love Thee more dearly, and
Follow Thee more nearly,
Day by day.
Amen.

Prayer Goals

Prayer Intentions

For whom or what do you want to pray this week? In particular, consider praying for those who frustrate or anger you, maybe even those who have harmed you or your loved ones.

_____
_____
_____
_____
_____
_____
_____

As St. (Mother) Teresa said, "Not all of us can do great things. But we can do ... *small things with great love*"

List your "small things" below:

_____
_____
_____
_____
_____
_____
_____
_____
_____

Goals Checklist

Don't feel like you need to check all these boxes every week. Start with a goal of perhaps 2 or 3 and build from there.

- ☐ Spiritual Reading
- ☐ Share your faith with someone
- ☐ Attend Church Services
- ☐ Pray with somebody
- ☐ Volunteer at Homeless Shelter or Food Bank
- ☐ Attend a Bible Study

Week Fifty-Two

first, Breathe

Breathe in ...
7 seconds.
Hold your breath ...
7 seconds.
Breathe out ...
7 seconds.

Repeat.

As many times as you like.

second, Become aware of God's Presence

third, Thanksgiving

Lord, I realize that all, even myself, is a gift from you. Today, for what things am I most grateful?

fourth, Reflect

Peace I leave with you; my peace I give to you; not as the world gives do I give to you. Let not your hearts be troubled, neither let them be afraid.
John 14:27

fifth, Examination

Lord, open my eyes and ears to be more honest with myself. Show me what has been happening to me and in me this day. Today, how have I experienced your love?

_____
_____
_____
_____
_____
_____
_____
_____
_____
_____

sixth, Contrition

Today, what choices have been inadequate responses to your love?

_____
_____
_____
_____
_____
_____
_____

seventh, Hope

Lord, let me look with longing toward the future. How will I let you lead me to a brighter tomorrow?

_____
_____
_____
_____
_____
_____
_____

Weekly Prayer

Holy Spirit Prayer of Saint Augustine

Breathe in me, O Holy Spirit,
That my thoughts may all be holy.
Act in me, O Holy Spirit,
That my work, too, may be holy.
Draw my heart, O Holy Spirit,
That I love but what is holy.
Strengthen me, O Holy Spirit,
To defend all that is holy.
Guard me, then, O Holy Spirit,
That I may always be holy.

Prayer Goals

Prayer Intentions

For whom or what do you want to pray this week? In particular, consider praying for those who frustrate or anger you, maybe even those who have harmed you or your loved ones.

_____
_____
_____
_____
_____
_____
_____
_____
_____

> As St. (Mother) Teresa said, "Not all of us can do great things. But we can do ... *small things with great love*"

List your "small things" below:

_____
_____
_____
_____
_____
_____
_____
_____
_____
_____

Goals Checklist

Don't feel like you need to check all these boxes every week. Start with a goal of perhaps 2 or 3 and build from there.

- [ ] Spiritual Reading
- [ ] Share your faith with someone
- [ ] Attend Church Services
- [ ] Pray with somebody
- [ ] Volunteer at Homeless Shelter or Food Bank
- [ ] Attend a Bible Study

About the Authors

Sara A. and Scott L. Smith are currently in the 9th year of their honeymoon. *Pray, Hope, & Don't Worry* is the first published collaboration from husband and wife writing team of Smith & Smith, though they have already written many stories for their four young children. The Smith family currently resides in their shared hometown of New Roads, Louisiana.

Sara A. Smith (who goes by her middle name "Ashton") received her degree in Creative Writing from Louisiana State University. She has published multiple short works of fiction on Catholic themes.

Scott L. Smith is an author, attorney, and theologian. Scott is a lover of all things Catholic: the Eucharist, the Blessed Mother, and especially the King of Kings, Who is the hidden connection between all history, Scripture, culture, and theology.

Check out more of his writing and courses below ...

More from Scott Smith

Scott regularly contributes to his blog, The Scott Smith Blog, WINNER of the 2018-2019 Fisher's Net Award for Best Catholic Blog, found at www.thescottsmithblog.com:

Scott's other books can be found at his publisher's, Holy Water Books, website, holywaterbooks.com, as well as on Amazon.

His other books on theology and the Catholic faith include *Pray the Rosary with St. John Paul II*, *The Catholic ManBook*, *Everything You Need to Know About Mary But Were Never Taught*, and *Blessed is He Who ...* (Biographies of Blesseds). More on these below ...

His fiction includes *The Seventh Word*, a pro-life horror novel, and the *Cajun Zombie Chronicles*, the Catholic version of the zombie apocalypse.

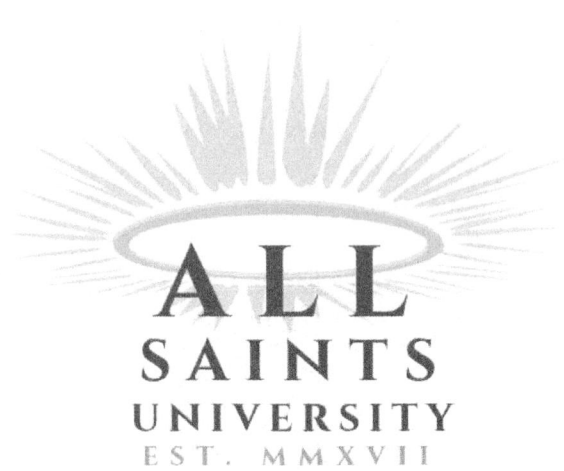

Scott has also produced courses on the Blessed Mother and Scripture for All Saints University.

Learn about the Blessed Mary from anywhere and learn to defend your mother! It includes over six hours of video plus a free copy of the next book ... Enroll Now!

What You Need to Know About Mary But Were Never Taught

Give a robust defense of the Blessed Mother using Scripture. Now, more than ever, every Catholic needs to learn how to defend their mother, the Blessed Mother. Because now, more than ever, the family is under attack and needs its Mother.

Discover the love story, hidden within the whole of Scripture, of the Father for his daughter, the Holy Spirit for his spouse, and the Son for his MOTHER.

This collection of essays and the All Saints University course made to accompany it will demonstrate through Scripture how the Immaculate Conception of Mary was prophesied in Genesis.

It will also show how the Virgin Mary is the New Eve, the New Ark, and the New Queen of Israel.

Pray the Rosary with St. John Paul II

St. John Paul II said "the Rosary is my favorite prayer." So what could possibly make praying the Rosary even better? Praying the Rosary with St. John Paul II! **This book includes a reflection from John Paul II for every mystery of the Rosary.** You will find John Paul II's biblical reflections on the twenty mysteries of the Rosary that provide practical insights to help you not only understand the twenty mysteries but also live them.

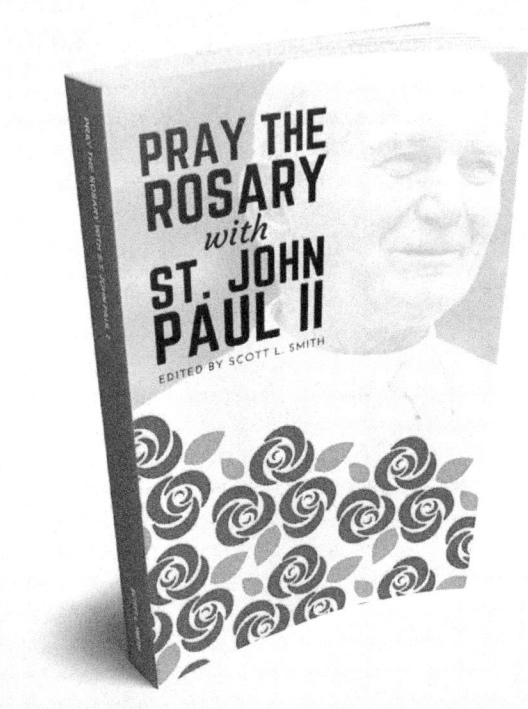

St. John Paul II said "The Rosary is my favorite prayer. Marvelous in its simplicity and its depth. In the prayer we repeat many times the words that the Virgin Mary heard from the Archangel, and from her kinswoman Elizabeth."

St. John Paul II said "the Rosary is the storehouse of countless blessings." In this new book, he will help you dig even deeper into the treasures contained within the Rosary.

You will also learn St. John Paul II's spirituality of the Rosary: "To pray the Rosary is to hand over our burdens to the merciful hearts of Christ and His mother."

"The Rosary, though clearly Marian in character, is at heart a Christ-centered prayer. It has all the depth of the gospel message in its entirety. It is an echo of the prayer of Mary, her perennial Magnificat for the work of the redemptive Incarnation which began in her virginal womb."

Take the Rosary to a whole new level with St. John Paul the Great! St. John Paul II, *pray for us*!

Catholic Nerds Podcast

As you might have noticed, Scott is obviously well-credentialed as a nerd. Check out Scott's podcast: the Catholic Nerds Podcast on iTunes, Podbean, Google Play, and wherever good podcasts are found!

The Catholic ManBook

Do you want to reach Catholic Man LEVEL: EXPERT? *The Catholic ManBook* is your handbook to achieving Sainthood, manly Sainthood. Find the following resources inside, plus many others:

- Top Catholic Apps, Websites, and Blogs
- Everything you need to pray the Rosary
- The Most Effective Daily Prayers & Novenas, including the Emergency Novena
- Going to Confession and Eucharistic Adoration like a boss!
- Mastering the Catholic Liturgical Calendar

The Catholic ManBook contains the collective wisdom of The Men of the Immaculata, of saints, priests and laymen, fathers and sons, single and married. Holiness is at your fingertips. Get your copy today.

NEW! This year's edition also includes a revised and updated St. Louis de Montfort Marian consecration. Follow the prayers in a day-by-day format.

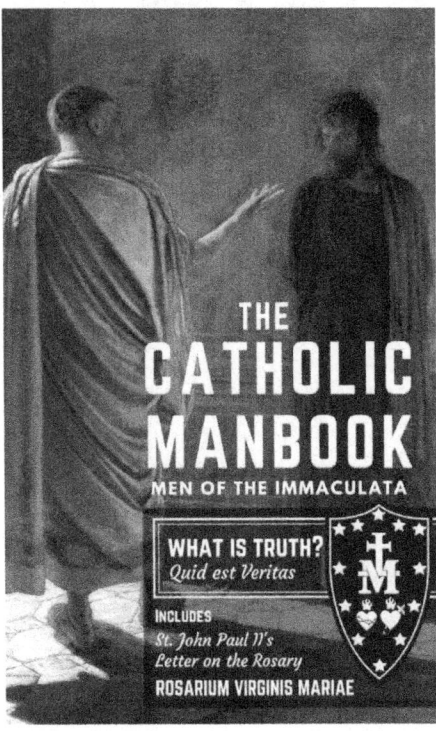
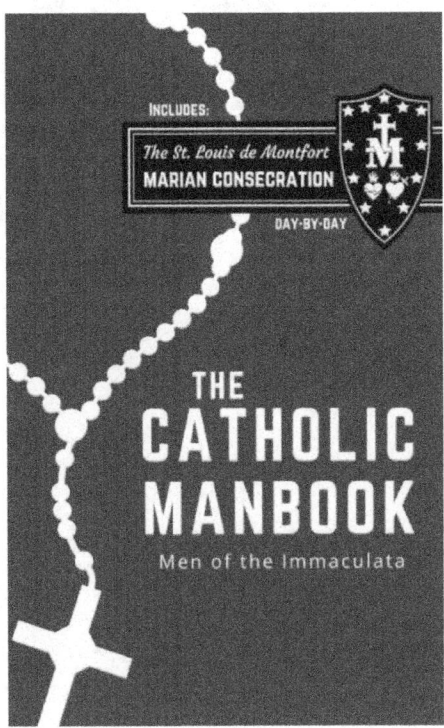

The Seventh Word

The FIRST Pro-Life Horror Novel!

Pro-Life hero, Abby Johnson, called it "legit scary ... I don't like reading this as night! ... It was good, it was so good ... it was terrifying, but good."

The First Word came with Cain, who killed the first child of man. The Third Word was Pharaoh's instruction to the midwives. The Fifth Word was carried from Herod to Bethlehem. One of the Lost Words dwelt among the Aztecs and hungered after their children.

Evil hides behind starched white masks. The ancient Aztec demon now conducts his affairs in the sterile environment of corporate medical facilities. An insatiable hunger draws the demon to a sleepy Louisiana hamlet. There, it contracts the services of a young attorney, Jim David, whose unborn child is the ultimate object of the demon's designs. Monsignor, a mysterious priest of unknown age and origin, labors unseen to save the soul of a small town hidden deep within Louisiana's plantation country, nearly forgotten in a bend of the Mississippi River.

You'll be gripped from start to heart-stopping finish in this page-turning thriller from new author S.L. Smith.

With roots in Bram Stoker's Dracula, this horror novel reads like Stephen King's classic stories of towns being slowly devoured by an unseen evil and the people who unite against it.

The book is set in southern Louisiana, an area the author brings to life with compelling detail based on his local knowledge.

Blessed is He Who ... Models of Catholic Manhood

You are the average of the five people you spend the most time with, so spend more time with the Saints! Here are several men that you need to get to know whatever your age or station in life. These short biographies will give you an insight into how to live better, however you're living.

From Kings to computer nerds, old married couples to single teenagers, these men gave us extraordinary examples of holiness:

- Pier Giorgio Frassati & Carlo Acutis - Here are two ex-traordinary **young men**, an athlete and a computer nerd, living on either side of the 20th Century
- Two men of royal stock, Francesco II and Archduke Eu-gen, lived lives of holiness despite all the world conspir-ing against them.
- There's also the **simple husband and father**, Blessed Luigi. Though he wasn't a king, he can help all of us treat the women in our lives as queens.

Blessed Is He Who ... Models of Catholic Manhood explores the lives of six men who found their greatness in Christ and His Bride, the Church. In six succinct chapters, the authors, noted historian Brian J. Costello and theologian and attorney Scott L. Smith, share with you the uncommon lives of exceptional men who will one day be numbered among the Saints of Heaven, men who can bring all of us closer to sainthood.

THANKS FOR READING!

Totus Tuus

Made in the USA
Coppell, TX
29 March 2020